RCM 3.23

Stand Your Ground

Stand Your Ground

An Introductory Text for Apologetics Students

DEAN HARDY

Wipf & Stock
PUBLISHERS
Eugene, Oregon

STAND YOUR GROUND
An Introductory Text for Apologetics Students

ISBN 10: 1-55635-104-6
ISBN 13: 978-1-55635-104-4

Manufactured in the U.S.A.

Dedicated to my beloved teachers:

Dana Bible
Norman Geisler
Richard Howe
Tom Howe

for the glory of God

Contents

Acknowledgements

I WOULD LIKE to recognize Jerry Meyer, Kari Cope, and Jarib Walden for their editing work and advice concerning this text.

Secondly, I also want to thank my main source of inspiration: my students. Without your passion for Christ and relentless inquisitiveness, this book would have been incomplete. Your questioning truly has made my faith stronger and prepared me to write this book.

Lastly, I thank Jennah, Thaddeus, and my entire family for your undying love and support.

Introduction

NOTHING IS more important in communicating Christ in today's world than apologetics, and no group has a greater need to receive this communication than our young people. The day has simply passed when we can just begin with the Gospel. The Good News of salvation through Christ presupposes so much that our culture rejects that we simply must address these first.

We cannot claim Christ is the Son of God unless our audience is convinced there is a God who can have a Son. Nor can we begin with the Word of God unless they believe there is a God who can speak such a Word. Further, we cannot even speak about our basic beliefs as objectively true unless there is such as thing as objective truth. Finally, all we believe is based on the supernatural. But there cannot be special acts of God unless there is a God who can perform these special acts. Therefore, the defense of absolute truth, the existence of God, and the viability of miracles are apologetic necessities in today's relativistic, agnostic, non-theistic, and naturalistic culture.

To put it succinctly, we need pre-evangelism today before we can do effective evangelism. Apologetics provides the crucial pre-evangelism needed. The most famous apologist of the twentieth century said it best:

> If all the world were Christian, it might not matter if all were uneducated. But, as it is, a cultural life will exist outside the church whether it exists inside or not. To be ignorant and simple now—not to be able to meet the enemies on their ground—would be to throw down our weapons, and to betray our uneducated brethren who have, under God, no defense but us against the intellectual attacks of the heathen. Good philosophy must exist, if for no other reason, because bad philosophy needs to be answered (C. S. Lewis, *The Weight of Glory*, 50).

This apologetics book for young people helps to fill this need for good philosophy. For unless we can answer the bad philosophy of our age into which our youth are being indoctrinated by the culture daily, we shall never be able to establish them in the good philosophy of Christianity.

The warning of the apostle Paul is as sharp today as it was in the first century when it was given: "Beware of philosophy . . . " (Col. 2:8). But one cannot be-ware of philosophy unless he is aware of philosophy. No one would go to a doctor for a cure who didn't study sickness. For how can one treat the illness unless he knows what it is? Likewise, our young people must be exposed to the ideological "diseases" of our day in order to know how to respond to them. This is precisely what this text does in an effective way.

Norman L. Geisler

Chapter 1

An Introduction to the Art of Apologetics

"What I am saying is true and reasonable."[1]
—The Apostle Paul

The Definition of Apologetics

APOLOGETICS IS the area of study purely devoted to the justification and defense of the Christian faith. Unlike American popular usage of the word "apology," the word apologetics has nothing to do with saying you're sorry. The word apologetics is derived from the Latin word *apologia* that does not imply an admission of guilt, but rather involves an attempt to clear the way for some line of reasoning. The goal of the apologist is to explain the reasoning behind Christianity to the unsaved in order to "clear the path to the cross."

Proving Christianity

It should be duly noted that the apologist's primary goal is not to "prove Christianity," but to justify and defend it. Peter made the definitive statement concerning apologetics: "Always be prepared to give an answer to everyone who asks you to give the reason for the hope that you have. But do this with gentleness and respect."[2] Our goal as apologists is not to prove Christianity, but to show that it is a credible religion. Of course, it would be amazing if at the end of a discussion the challenger asks, "How do I become a Christian?" But it must be realized that your primary purpose is to clearly show the challenger that the basic truths of Christianity are possible, if not probable.

---

[1] Acts 26:25.
[2] 1 Pet. 3:15.

Apologetics should be considered under the heading of **pre-evangelism**.[3] When you begin an apologetic discussion, the questioner generally believes that "Christianity cannot be true because of x, y, and z." Your hope should be that when the discussion ends, and when "x, y, and z" have been dealt with, the listener then wonders, "Maybe Christianity is true!" Just like all other types of pre-evangelism, the result rarely ends in immediate conversion, but the apologist always hopes and prays that he has made the way clear for further spiritual development of the unsaved.

As an example, let's look at a topic that had conspiracy theorists and NASA officials agitated. In 2001 the Fox TV network aired a one-hour program called "Conspiracy Theory: Did We Land on the Moon?" The television show hypothesized that NASA's Apollo missions to the moon were in fact fraudulent and that the moon landings were actually filmed here on earth. Admittedly, for someone who lacks knowledge in astronomy, the filmmakers had some pretty convincing points. Why did the flag planted on the moon's surface wave if there was no wind? Why were there no stars in the background of the photographs? I remember talking to a few friends the next day and a few of them were convinced that we never landed on the moon! Luckily, a few independent astronomers and NASA put out a rebuttal discussing each and every one of the arguments laid out against the moon landings throughout the television show.

What do NASA and an apologist have in common? Both have to defend what they believe to be truth. Defending truth would be easy if you could simply send someone back in time to see for himself. But unfortunately, not even NASA can send people back in time to see with their own eyes the moon landings or even Jesus' resurrection. It is simply impossible. Instead, each must rationally defend a past series of events in order to show that their beliefs have solid foundations. NASA showed that the waving flag was due to the astronauts twisting the flag into the moon rock. Christians must show that it is logical to believe the notion that God exists. NASA explained the problems with space photography. Christians must defend the authority and historicity of the Bible. In the same way NASA defended its work, we must be able to defend our faith.

At the end of my first year teaching apologetics, I had a very interesting discussion with a student. Once I had reached the end of all of the

---

[3] Pre-evangelism is merely the term denoting events or ideas that lead up to the explanation of the gospel. Sometimes pre-evangelism is simply the bond of trust that needs to be built between the Christian and non-Christian. Other times pre-evangelism is used in regards to the intellectual barriers that have formed between a non-Christian and the tenets of Christianity.

lessons and given all of my arguments and presentations, the student had the nerve to state, "You just can't prove Christianity." I had discussed every issue in this textbook with this student and he still thought that I had not proven Christianity. Yet after further dialogue, I understood what the student was suggesting and realized that he was correct! He simply was stating that no one could prove with mathematical certainty that Christianity is true.

The point of this example is that the student of apologetics should not be expected to prove Christianity "without a shadow of a doubt." But rather, the student should be able to convey that Christianity is free from contradiction and that the doctrines therein are reasonable.

Do not be confused, there is proof that Christianity is true; but the proofs laid out in this book will not result in 100% assurance. The proofs for God's existence, the historical evidence, and the reliability of the Bible have the potential to convince someone that Christianity is real, but they will never result in proof with logical certainty. These proofs are like pieces of an intricate puzzle. It takes many different shaped pieces to make the puzzle complete. In the same way, the proof for Christianity is made of many different arguments, but when they all come together they result in a fairly persuasive line of reasoning. But remember, no matter how convincing your arguments are, there must always be room for faith.

Defending and giving proof for the credibility of Christianity are the two oars of the apologetic rowboat. While mathematical proof is never an option, the arguments for the existence of God and the reasonableness of Christianity are very persuasive and should be fully grasped so that they may be utilized in any apologetic situation.

Why Study Apologetics?

One of the major complaints of students is that the information that they are learning in school seems impractical. Whether in college or in kindergarten, there is always one student who has to ask the infamous question, "When am I going to use this in real life?" The question is actually a very valid one. If the information that is being taught in class does not contribute to your well-being as a person or will not be needed in a real-life situation, then why should you spend your energy learning it?

It seems that apologetics qualifies as a subject that is worthy of study. Both of the above qualifications are fulfilled. Apologetics will help your spiritual well-being as well as give you information that will later be used in real life situations. It will help you become more analytical of the world around you, determine what you see and hear to be true or false, and intelligently converse with those who have different opinions. If you are not convinced, here are three major reasons why studying apologetics is worthy of your time and effort:

1) Defend the Christian Faith

If you are an American from a Christian background, it is very likely that you haven't been subjected to the ideas of anti-Christians. Many times parents shelter their children so that they will not be subject to the opinions of those who openly disagree with the Christian worldview. Generally, it is not until the child reaches the college campus when he completely comes out from under the shelter that the parents have constructed. Once on campus, the parents are no longer directly involved in the protection of the mind and soul of their child. Unfortunately, it also seems that colleges and universities, even Christian institutions, are places where divergent and unorthodox beliefs are spawned and cultivated. No matter if you are a high school student who is looking forward to college, or already a member of a higher learning institution, the shelter your parents built will be left and you will have to protect yourself against the barrage of anti-Christian beliefs.

It seems as though these attacks can be divided into three separate groups: atheists, different religions, and seekers. The atheists, or those who reject any concept of the supernatural, are the most ornery of the three. For example, take this statement by atheist Bertrand Russell in his book *Why I am not a Christian*, "I think that all the great religions of the world—Buddhism, Hinduism, Christianity, Islam, and Communism— both untrue and harmful [*sic*]."[4] The corrosiveness of the atheistic movement can be easily observed in Russell's statement. Not only does he believe Christianity to be illogical and false, but he also claims that it is harmful. Regrettably, Russell is not alone. There is no doubt that you will eventually run into a person that completely denies the existence of God and is belligerent toward the Christian religion.

While Christianity is the largest religious movement in the world, there are a very large percentage of people who are involved in other religious movements with which you are likely to come in contact. Whether the person is of a completely different world religion or an offshoot of Christianity, there will always be an opportunity to explain why you believe in the Christian worldview. If you haven't already, it will be to your advantage to take a class in world religions and/or cults in order to under-

---

[4] Bertrand Russell, *Why I am not a Christian* (New York: Simon and Schuster, 1957), v.

stand the beliefs that oppose orthodox Christianity. This will not only help you understand other religions, but will also show you how to lovingly point out the contradictions that lie within them.

Lastly, there will be those who are simply seeking truth and may have questions about Christianity. In general, seekers are sitting on the fence of religion. They haven't made a decision regarding what to believe and hopefully you may have a hand in dealing with the difficulties they have with Christianity. This is generally where apologetics and evangelism collide, and is the subject of the last chapter of this book.

2) To Protect and Develop your Personal Faith

One of the secondary roles of apologetics, and a major role in the motivation for writing this book, is for the personal protection and development of the faith of the young-adult Christian. It seems that young adulthood is one of the most tumultuous times in regards to one's faith. Katie, a strong Christian and a college freshman writes, "I went to [college] feeling totally ready, excited to just get away and do something new and exciting, not realizing that I was entering into the most intense battle I've experienced yet in life. Spiritually, mentally, relationally . . . in every aspect . . . my freshman year of college was a battle."[5]

All one needs to do to see this problem firsthand is to consult a few churches, or better yet, visit the college ministry at your own church. Many churches do not even have college ministries! It seems that the church's biggest shortcoming is not serving the college-aged group. The George Barna research group states that, "Millions of twenty-something Americans—many of whom were active in churches during their teens—pass through their most formative adult decade while putting Christianity on the backburner."[6] Why does this happen? Tom Bisset, the author of *Why Christian Kids Leave the Faith* writes that what causes confusion among young adults is that they "have troubling, unanswered questions about their faith," and that "they never personally owned their own faith."[7] Hopefully, your study of apologetics will take care of both of these problems.

---

[5] Katie Baucom, to Dean Hardy, 2 June 2005, transcript in the hand of Dean Hardy.

[6] George Barna, "Twentysomethings Struggle to Find Their Place in Christian Churches" internet, http://www.barna.org/FlexPage.aspx?Page=BarnaUpdate&BarnaUpdateID=149.

[7] Tom Bisset, *Why Christian Kids Leave the Faith* (Grand Rapids: Discovery House, 1997), table of contents.

3) Because God's Word tells us to!

To some, the defense of Christianity seems a little unnecessary. Does God really need to be defended? Of course not! An omnipotent being needs no security guard. Yet in the same sense that David defended the name of God against the slander of Goliath, we too are called to stand up and defend God, his Word, and Christianity as a whole. As 1 Peter 3:15 says, we are to "Always be prepared to give an answer to everyone who asks you to give the reason for the hope that you have." Each and every Christian should be willing and ready to stand up for Christ, and explain why we believe in the Gospel.

The Bible is peppered with instances where the apostles vigorously defended the truth of the Gospel. There is no doubt that the apostle who did most to spread the Gospel of Jesus Christ was Paul of Tarsus. One of the most famous apologetic events in the Bible happened during Paul's trip to Athens: "While Paul was waiting for them in Athens, he was greatly distressed to see that the city was full of idols. So he reasoned in the synagogue with the Jews and the God-fearing Greeks, as well as in the marketplace day by day with those who happened to be there."[8] Paul saw the need and the opportunity to share the gospel with the Jews and Gentiles in Athens. This was not an easy evangelistic mission. Paul entered into a place where the community believed in a plethora of gods, not merely the God of Abraham, Isaac, and Jacob. He had to explain Christianity in a way that they could understand, while not offending them to the point where they would banish him from the city.

There is no doubt that Paul believed that defending the gospel was necessary. In 2 Corinthians 10:5 Paul writes, "We *demolish arguments* and every pretension that sets itself up against the knowledge of God, and we take captive every thought to make it obedient to Christ." Again in Philippians 1:7, "It is right for me to feel this way about all of you, since I have you in my heart; for whether I am in chains or *defending and confirming the gospel,* all of you share in God's grace with me." Paul, who unapologetically proclaimed the good news, saw the need for apologetics along with evangelism. He understood that some non-Christians would have intellectual barriers between them and the Lord. He sought to knock down those walls so that the pathway to Christ would be clear. In the same way Paul desired to win over the Athenians, we should be inclined to win our friends and neighbors.

---

[8] Acts 17:16–17.

The Challenge of Apologetics

If you have ever been to a Christian conference where evangelism was a topic, you may remember leaving the convention invigorated and charged to spread the Gospel. Unfortunately, our emotional states waver from the "mountain-top experience" and soon after, the feelings fade away. When the passion is gone we are much less likely to act on what we have learned. There must be more to evangelism than merely hearing a speaker and getting excited. Evangelism takes work. In the same way, it should be realized that the study of apologetics is not an effortless endeavor. You cannot simply read this book or listen to a teacher's lecture and become an effective apologist. There simply must be more than that! The following are areas where the effective apologist excels: Intellectual Activity, a Passion for Christ, and Bravery.

Intellectual Activity—It seems as though some churches have a vendetta against scholars. This hostility is likely due to the fact that most people who criticize Christianity are "intellectuals." Thus the community of Christians incorrectly fuses the concept of intelligence with the arrogance of atheism. Yet it seems that Christians who neglect the intellect are throwing out the baby with the bathwater. If God gave us minds to use, why shouldn't we use them to help show others the credibility of Christianity? In fact, it seems that if we let our minds go to waste, we may be doing the opposite of what God wants us to do. Just as a muscle will atrophy if it is not exercised, the mind will be wasted if it is not applied.

It may be the case that this poison called **anti-intellectualism**[9] may actually be more than a fad, but may be more of an adopted lifestyle. J. P. Moreland and William Lane Craig in their *Philosophical Foundations for a Christian Worldview* write, "Our churches are unfortunately overly populated with people whose minds, as Christians, are going to waste . . . they may be spiritually regenerate, but their minds have not been converted; they still think like nonbelievers. Despite their Christian commitment, they remain largely empty selves. What is an empty self? An empty self is a person who is passive, sensate, busy and hurried, incapable of developing an interior life. Such a person is inordinately individualistic, infantile and narcissistic."[10]

---

[9] Since most atheists are scholars, some church members presuppose that all scholars are atheists.

[10] J. P. Moreland and William Lane Craig, *Philosophical Foundations for a Christian Worldview* (Downers Grove: Intervarsity Press, 2003), 5.

Two points in the above statement about the membership of the church seem the most critical: "a person who is passive" and "incapable of developing an interior life." As Christians we cannot be passive. We cannot sit on the sideline. There wouldn't be a story about David and Goliath if David hadn't jumped into battle. But this statement is even deeper than this analogy. As Christians we cannot be passive *intellectually*. We must be actively pursing truth and *learning*. The more you know about the truth of Christianity and the beliefs of the worldviews that reject our faith, the more you will be able to defend your commitment to Christ. Secondly, Moreland and Craig warn that some Christians are "incapable of developing an interior life." What they mean by that statement is that we have become so overwhelmed by the stresses and distractions of life; we do not have the time or even the intentions of developing a spiritual life. This leads us to our next major point.

A Passion for Christ—Of course, if there is no passion for Jesus, then the motivation for action is non-existent. What should be our motivation?, love. We should passionately love our Savior for what he has done for us. It seems that in both Old and New Testaments the connection between love and obedience is realized. Deuteronomy 11:1 states "Love the LORD your God and keep his requirements, his decrees, his laws and his commands always." In the New Testament there is the memorable exchange between Jesus and Peter in John 21:15, "When they had finished eating, Jesus said to Simon Peter, 'Simon son of John, do you truly love me more than these?' 'Yes, Lord,' he said, 'you know that I love you.' Jesus said, 'Feed my lambs.'" In both of these cases love seemed to be the cause of the obedience. If we truly love Christ with a passion, each and every one of us should be doing his will. Remember the words of John, "By this we know that we love the children of God, when we love God, and keep his commandments. For this is the love of God, that we keep his commandments: and his commandments are not grievous."[11]

Bravery—Of course, if you love God and are intellectually active, but are not willing to stand your ground, then you will lack effectiveness as an apologist and an evangelist. Ephesians 6:13 reads, "Therefore put on the full armor of God, so that when the day of evil comes, you may be able to stand your ground, and after you have done everything, to stand." We have to be able to break free of our comfort zones and speak up. There will be times where it may be necessary to say something in opposition to a professor during class. Maybe you will need to stand your ground against

[11] 1 John 5:2–3.

a fellow student who is an antagonistic atheist. Wherever the case, you need to be brave and *Stand your Ground!* Of course, the results of this action may vary. You may make a valid point, or miss the point completely. Either way, you may fear embarrassment, but remember, that embarrassment will be nothing like the physical abuse that was administered to the disciples. Peter reminds us, "Who is going to harm you if you are eager to do good? But even if you should suffer for what is right, you are blessed. Do not fear what they fear; do not be frightened."[12] No matter the result, God will be pleased that you stood your ground.

The Four Types of Christian Apologetics

While the many different classifications of the types of apologetics are as numerous as the authors who write about them, they have been narrowed here into four distinct categories. These types of apologetics should not be regarded as all-inclusive or rigid classes, but rather as the types of basic argumentation that people use when defending Christianity. It will be shown that some are more effective than others, while one stands above the rest as the most functional.

Presuppositional Apologetics

Examination—A presuppositional apologist generally asserts that Christianity should be proven on the grounds of some basic, fundamental assumptions. They assume that the listener and the apologist agree on the same set of presuppositions. Of course, there are many sorts of presuppositional apologists who have different sets of assumptions, but the most widely held presumptions by these apologists are that the Christian God exists and the Word of God is true.

There is no doubt that everyone has presuppositions. Whether you are discussing what type of dog to bring into your home or what type food to have for dinner, there are all sorts of presuppositions that come into play in every decision. Did you have a bad experience with a Doberman when you were a child? If so, you probably won't want that type of dog in your home. You simply have assumed, based on one event, that Dobermans are bad dogs. If you once had a good experience at a Chinese restaurant, you may assume that all Chinese restaurants have good food. Presuppositions are impossible to overlook. Yet with the presuppositional apologist, he knows these presuppositions are there and contends that the non-Christian must

---

[12] 1 Pet. 3:14.

adhere to his presuppositions before any further developments can take place. For instance, if he comes into contact with an atheist, no further discussion can be had until the atheist holds the same presuppositions as the apologist. Generally speaking, the presuppositionalist sees no room for logical arguments.

There is no intention here to portray the presuppositionalist as arrogant or dogmatic; rather, once one understands his reasons, one may gain insight into his views. Generally, most who hold to this view do so because they believe that man is in such a fallen state that he cannot successfully understand the basic truths of Christianity. The only way one accepts these truths is through the work of the Holy Spirit. They use 1 Corinthians 2:14 as an example: "The man without the Spirit does not accept the things that come from the Spirit of God, for they are foolishness to him, and he cannot understand them, because they are spiritually discerned." Thus, only God can bring someone to realize that the Trinity exists and that the Scripture is true; no man can bring a non-believer to that state.

Critique—As it has been shown, the presuppositionalist approach to apologetics is founded on the concept that the mind is completely fallen to the point that humanity is incapable of using reason to come to the truth about Christianity. This will be discussed in more detail in the next chapter, but for now it must be concluded that while reason is by no means flawless, it is neither completely destroyed. Rationality is one of the traits that distinguish us from the animals that roam the earth. Humans can think and come to their own conclusions on such important issues as politics, morality, and religion and many unimportant issues such as what one wants for lunch, or what color socks would match one's pants. No matter the case, every healthy person in every decision uses reason.

Secondly, it seems that the presuppositional view of apologetics is the least effective of the four. Many of the people you will come across in this world will not have the same presuppositions that you have. Millions come from different backgrounds and worldviews emerging from countries across the globe. Should one simply quote Scripture to these lost and dying souls? If you are trying to defend the Christian faith, yet you simply shrug off an atheist's claims, what good have you done? On the other hand, if there was a chance you could convince, or at least interest a person in the idea that Christianity may be true by using reason, it seems that you should attempt to use this ability to bring that person to Christ. Nonetheless, it cannot be assumed that the presuppositionalist is completely incorrect, for many have come to Christ by their efforts. Yet many of those, if not all, had to have already believed that there is a God and that the Bible is true.

Experiential Apologetics

Examination—The experiential apologist attempts to defend Christianity by giving account of his personal experiences with God. This type of apologetics is often found among the members of the Pentecostal denominations across the world. These groups generally stress the importance of supernatural experiences with the Holy Spirit and the resurrected Christ. When an outsider questions the credibility of Christianity these experiences are relied on to justify the faith of the believer.

The use of logic and reasoning take a back seat in this type of apologetics. Most in this camp would claim that an experience with God is much more convincing and real than any argument can possibly be. Thus, if an experience is more effective, why even consider using arguments?

Critique—It seems that the experiential apologists may be accurate when it is said that experience is more convincing than logic. This is the reason why math teachers use apples and oranges to prove that two plus two really does equal four. While there may be some truth that personal experience is beneficial, two things must be considered.

First, we cannot force God into an experience with an atheist, or vice versa. If it were that easy to simply "show God" to an atheist, there would likely be many less atheists in the world. Secondly, a person must believe that a thing exists prior to believing that another person had an experience with it. For example, if one claims to have seen and experienced a unicorn, you would not believe unless you saw this unicorn for yourself. Even if you were approached by a whole group of unicorn enthusiasts who claim to have seen unicorns, you would still be skeptical about their claims. You would simply think that these people were either misguided, playing a joke, or simply insane. Unfortunately, this is the same conclusion that an atheist assumes when conversing with a Christian. The atheist thinks, "There is no God, so this Christian must be misguided, or simply insane." The atheist doesn't believe God exists, so he doesn't buy the experiential testimony of the Christian.

While the experiences claimed by an experiential apologist can be real and sometimes very believable, it is very tough to convince a skeptic using this line of reasoning. The apologetic value of another person's experience is modest at best.

Evidential Apologetics

Examination—The evidential apologist seeks to use physical evidence, guided by reason, to defend and give credence to the Christian faith. The apologist uses Christian and secular historical documents as well as archaeological finds to defend the faith.

One of the most widely known adherents to this system is author and speaker Josh McDowell. He travels the world to promote a Christian lifestyle, most usually directed to young people and their parents. In the seventies McDowell put out a historic apologetic work entitled *Evidence that Demands a Verdict*. In the book he first attempts to prove the reliability of the Bible, then continues on to prove that Jesus was who he said he was. The book is an invaluable asset to any Christian and should be among the library of any serious apologist. However, it will be noticed that there is something missing from his book: any arguments for God's existence. The historical apologist simply does not see the need for proving the existence of God before moving on to other evidences. They believe that the historical evidence alone is adequate to convince a skeptic.

Critique—While the evidential apologist is fairly successful in his apologetic endeavors, he often finds it difficult when a staunch atheist or agnostic confronts him. It seems that the historical apologist is limiting the tools that he can utilize to defend his faith. While it is true that most of America believes that there is a supernatural force that exists in this universe, many of those do not believe in the God of the Bible, and unfortunately, there is a portion of them that do not believe in God at all. The historical apologist would have a tough time effectively communicating with an atheist or even someone in the New Age movement. You may be able to prove that certain things in Christianity are historical; but, because someone else may hold a different worldview, he will interpret these facts in a different way than a Christian would. What is needed is something to help the skeptic understand our worldview, as well as our specific religion.

Classical Apologetics

Examination—The classical apologist also sees the need for historical and archaeological evidence; but unlike the evidential apologist, the classical apologist finds it necessary to begin with the proofs for the existence of God before moving on to other evidence. It seems that the classical approach is exactly like the evidential approach yet with the addition of these theistic arguments. Thus the classical approach prepares the student for almost every attack that can be leveled against the Christian. The atheist, agnostic, cult member, Muslim, and all other types of opponents of the faith can be resisted and possibly converted.

Dr. Norman Geisler in his *Baker Encyclopedia of Christian Apologetics* explains, "No rational person steps in an elevator without some reason to believe it will hold him up. No reasonable person gets on an airplane that is missing part of one wing and smells of smoke in the cabin . . . the rational person wants evidence that God exists before he places his faith in God. Rational unbelievers want evidence that Jesus is the Son of God before they place their trust in him."[13] It must be realized that the skeptic may have an intellectual barrier between him and God. The Christian community needs to be willing and able to remove those barriers and give the skeptic the reasons to believe that God exists. Due to the ability to reach the most people, it seems that the classical approach is the most effective system of apologetics, and the system that will be used throughout this book.

Summary

The art of apologetics is one that demands the attention of the evangelical Christian. In this world of desperation and hopelessness, one needs to be able not only to explain his faith, but also defend what he believes against the onslaught of intellectual attacks. Depending on your situation, you may not immediately see the use for apologetics, but there is no doubt that it will come in handy before long. Recently, a high school student returned to visit me after his first year in the army. Even though he was not one of my best students, he returned to tell me that his apologetics class was the most important class he took his senior year. The reason for this confession was due to the fact that in the army he was placed in a room with a Muslim. The roommates became friends and have had multiple discussions about the validity of Christianity. Of course, the Muslim was not instantly converted, but this recent graduate is making the way clear for this Muslim to come to Christ. Before he left he reminded me that it should be the goal of every Christian, to "go and make disciples of all nations."[14] *Stand your Ground* is intended to help prepare you for this objective, and to guide you toward fulfilling it.

[13] Norman Geisler, *Baker Encyclopedia of Christian Apologetics* (Grand Rapids: Baker Books, 1999), 38.

[14] Matt. 28:19.

Study Questions

1. Using your own wording, define and explain the art of apologetics.
2. In your own opinion, why do you feel that apologetics is worthy of study? How do you hope that this class will help you?
3. Is it the role of the apologist to "prove Christianity with 100% certainty"? Explain your answer.
4. Out of the three characteristics of an effective apologist (Intellectual Activity, a Passion for Christ, Bravery) which do you believe is your strongest characteristic? Which is your weakest? Why?
5. Compare and contrast the four different types of apologetics.

Terms to Consider

Apologetics
Pre-evangelism
Anti-intellectualism
Presuppositional Apologetics
Experiential Apologetics
Evidential Apologetics
Classical Apologetics

Memory Verse Options

1 Peter 3:15
2 Corinthians 10:5

Going Beyond the Call of Duty: Readings for the Overachiever

Geisler, Norman. *Baker Encyclopedia of Christian Apologetics.* Grand Rapids: Baker Books, 1999.

Moreland, J. P. and William Lane Craig. *Philosophical Foundations for a Christian Worldview.* Downers Grove: Intervarsity Press, 2003.

Chapter 2

Reality, Faith and Reason

"These are a shadow of the things that were to come;
the reality, however, is found in Christ."[1]
—The Apostle Paul

Is This World Real?

HAVE YOU ever seen a motion picture that changed your outlook on the world? Have you ever been so absorbed in a movie that when the lights came up at the end of the film, you actually felt slightly depressed that it ended? If you have, you have fully actualized the director's dream. The director's goal is to create a world where the audience member loses himself in the story. Oliver Stone, the director of such movies as *Platoon* and *JFK* contends that, "Film is a powerful medium. Film is a drug. Film is a potential hallucinogen. It goes into your eye. It goes into your brain. It stimulates. And it's a dangerous thing. It can be a very subversive thing."[2] The director hopes that the spectator becomes more than a spectator, he becomes a part of the story. He becomes so involved that he worries about the hero's future and wishes for the demise of the villain. The director's desire is that you forget reality and dive into an alternate and fictional one, even if it is only for a few hours.

Recently, Hollywood has produced some movies that have posed some very deep philosophical questions. One of the most successful movies was called *The Matrix*. For those who have seen the first of the three movies, you will remember that the premise revolved around the concept that the world most people thought was real wasn't real at all, but was merely a program. The *real* world was a world where the machines were supreme and the humans were oppressed and harvested for their energy.

[1] Col. 2:17.
[2] Taken from an interview with Oliver Stone on BBC's television show "Panorama."

The movie left you with a question to answer, "Is this world really real?" Of course, it is likely that most people shrugged off the question. After leaving the theater some may have jokingly pretended to question whether an object was real, while some may have even lightheartedly pointed out people that looked like 'agents'; but the fact of the matter is that whether this was an easy question for you to answer or not, the question requires an answer. Is this world real?

It may be surprising to some that there are actually people in the world who do not believe that this world is real. For example, there is a very interesting principle in Hinduism called *maya*. The basic concept behind this belief is that the world is an illusion. Renowned Christian apologist Norman Geisler explains, "The world that we see, hear, touch, taste, and smell does not actually exist. It appears to exist, but it is in fact an illusion, or *maya*. The universe we perceive is like walking through a dense forest at night and seeing what appears to be a snake. But when we return to the same spot in the light of the day, we see that the snake really was a rope. The rope looked like a snake, but it actually was not a snake. Just as the snake appeared to exist, so the universe appears to exist but it actually does not. Instead, the universe is *maya*, an illusion superimposed upon the only true reality, Brahman."[3] For Hindus, what is actually real is their transcendent deity named Brahman; the world is merely an illusion emanated by this supreme deity.

Of course, most people believe that the world actually exists, that these words are really printed on this page, and that the heart that thumps in your chest isn't a figment or an illusion. The point is simply that there is a percentage of the world that does not view the world in the same way we do. Eventually, we need to be able to explain what we believe to be real and why we believe these things exist.

What is Metaphysics?

It should be pointed out that the term "metaphysics" does have a variety of meanings. If you walk into your local bookstore and wander to the metaphysics section, you will not find books on Aristotle's *Metaphysics* or Aquinas' *Being and Essence*; rather, you would find books pertaining to astrology, the occult, and possibly even black magic. Recently, the occultists have adopted the term "metaphysics" and use it literally: meaning "beyond the physical." On the other hand, when the term "metaphysics"

[3] Geisler, Norman L., *Baker Encyclopedia of Christian Apologetics* (Baker Books: Grand Rapids), 1999.

is used by the student to his parent, or to a student not familiar with the branch of philosophy which it indicates, the term should then be clarified or the listener may believe that the student has fallen into occultism or some new age cult.[4]

Our designated definition for **metaphysics** is the following: *The science in which the nature of being, existence, and reality are investigated.* The metaphysician questions what things are real and how they exist. The scientist examines the realm of the physical, while the metaphysician asks, "What makes these physical things exist?"

The ancient philosopher Aristotle wrote, "This science is quite distinct from what we may call the special sciences, none of which investigates Being in its purely general aspect as Being, but each of which rather cuts off some partial aspect of Being and studies the set of properties belonging to that partial aspect."[5] For instance, Aristotle would consider physics as the branch of science that investigates Being as it is physically actual, and math would be the branch of science that investigates Being insomuch as it is quantifiable. But metaphysics is the study of Being as Being; Being in and of itself.[6]

Metaphysics is not limited to the nature of physical reality, but also supernatural reality. Generally, most metaphysicians understand the need for a deity in their system, or at least some sort of transcendent cause. Even Aristotle needed an "unmoved mover" to make his system of metaphysics work. Now, what Aristotle describes as "God" does not fit the description of the God of Isaac, Abraham, and Jacob, so you should not immediately assume that the philosophers are speaking of the same God in whom we believe. Nonetheless, the issue of the existence of the supernatural is not a major issue in metaphysics. What is a major issue is the nature of this supernatural being, especially his relationship to Being. The metaphysician wants to answer the question, "What's the role of the supernatural in the creation and continual existence of the universe?"

---

[4] To find the topic of this chapter in your local bookstore, you would need to peruse the philosophy section for Aristotle, and probably the religion section to find Aquinas.

[5] Aristotle, *Metaphysics*, vol. 8, in *Great Books of the Western World*, ed. Robert Maynard Hutchins (Chicago: Encyclopedia Britannica, 1952), 1003a17–25.

[6] "Being" here is not used as a noun such as: "human being", but rather as a verb. Being is not a thing, but rather an act. Synonymous with the term "Being" is the word "existence." When it is said that you have existence, it is not used the same way as when you say that you have hair. Being is the *act of existing over a period of time*. Simply put, if something has "Being": it *is*.

In review, the science of metaphysics boils down to two questions: "What is real?" and, "What makes it exist, rather than not exist?" The rest of the chapter will consider the first of these two questions, while the second will be set-aside for a more advanced pursuit. We must then determine what is real and the principles needed for such a mission.

Idealism vs. Realism

There are two sides of the coin when it comes to metaphysical study: Idealism and Realism. In basic terms, **metaphysical realism** presupposes that there is an external world that exists independently of your mind. If you observe an object, that object really does exist in the real world. Conversely, **idealism** generally rejects any existence of a material substance that exists apart from the mind. Thus we can assert that the only things that are real to an idealist are the ideas that exist in the mind.

As an example of idealism, take the philosophy of the sixteenth century Irish bishop George Berkeley. Berkeley is widely known for two axioms, the first of which was actually not stated by him but was asked by one of his students: "If a tree falls in the forest and no one is there to hear it, does it make a sound?" To a realist, the answer would be yes. Because a real tree fell to the ground, real noise was made. Scientifically, we could posit that there was evidence that proves that real sound was produced from the event. Using the **principle of uniformity**,[7] it can be asserted that since we have seen multiple trees fall and make sounds, then this falling tree was no different. Yet Berkeley disagreed. In fact, if we apply his philosophy correctly, not only did the tree not make a sound, but the tree itself did not exist. His second axiom further explains his philosophy: "To be is to be perceived." In his view, the only thing that is real is the sensation or perception that is in the mind; the external world has no existence in and of itself. The perception or idea of the object is what is real.

At this point, you simply need to ask yourself if realism is more credible than idealism. It seems as though only one of these options gives us the possibility of knowing an absolute reality, therefore we will presuppose metaphysical realism; the concept that there are things that really exist outside of ourselves. If this were not the case, our discussion of Christianity

---

[7] Principle of Uniformity- an observed cause that has produced the same observed effect many times over likely produced that same effect in the past, as well as will produce the same effect in the future. Experimental Science is built on this principle, for when an experiment is concluded it is supposed that the same experiment (cause) will produce the same result (effect). Another example is medicine; the doctor knows that if a certain medicine caused a biological effect in one patient, it will likely do the same for another.

and this entire book would have to stop here. If we could not be sure if our statements and ideas correspond to a real thing, then there could be no such thing as truth or knowledge.[8]

"One's whole life revolves around what they believe to be real."

Our view of what is real should shape our behavior. For example, if a man stands on a table in a crowded train station and yells, "I have a bomb!" how would most people react? Of course, most would attempt to get out of the station as fast as possible. In the same way, when a driver sees a fallen tree in the path, he generally does not ignore his senses and ram it. He slowly approaches the tree and decides the best way to get around it. He believes that the tree is real and that this real problem needs real solutions in order to reach a real conclusion.

Of course, the italicized statement above is most effective when considering one's supernatural beliefs. For instance, the thinker asks, "Is there really a God out there who is watching me? Is this God a moral lawgiver who will judge my actions?" If not, then the person's actions do not have eternal consequences and he can do whatever he wants. Yet if there is a God, the person needs to respect the rules that God has laid down for his protection. In the same way, when Jesus speaks to us through God's word, if we do believe it to be real, we should respond to that truth and take action when necessary.

The statement above is not merely a religious statement; it is also a general one. For instance, if your friend Bill tells you that there will be a birthday party at his house Friday night at eight o'clock and you accept the invitation, then you really do expect a party to be occurring on Friday night. You are certain that Bill's invitation was genuinely real. Now let us suppose that Bill was lying, or distorting the truth, or playing a practical joke; no matter, there really wasn't a party at his house. The reason why you will be mad at Bill is because what you believed to be real and what actually was real did not correspond. You really did believe the party and the invitation to be real, but unfortunately your belief was not supported. You will blame Bill because he was the reason why you believed.

---

[8] See the "foundation pyramid" in Chapter Four.

Why do you Believe What you Believe?

When I was in college I was confronted by a serious problem in my faith. I did not know it was a problem and, possibly, if I had lived the rest of my life in a cabin in the woods, the problem may have never reared its ugly head. I could have lived my entire life without noticing it.

The problem was my personal answer to a simple question: "Why do you believe what you believe?" Now if I was asked my freshman year of college why I believed what I believed, I would have given the Sunday school answer: "because I asked Jesus in my heart." Let it be known that this is not an incorrect answer! In fact, I would claim that it is most satisfactory. But the truth of the matter was that the main reason why I was a Christian and why I believed in Jesus was that my parents taught me to be a Christian. To this day I will contend that I was a Christian when I accepted Christ at age nine. I prayed to God in Jesus' name, read my Bible, went to church, and helped at my youth group. I truly had a personal relationship with Jesus. Yet I will also admit that I did not fully accept "Christianity" until my freshman year of college.

You may ask, "Well, what was the difference?" The difference is immense. In one case I simply believed on the authority of my parents, my youth pastor, and some of my friends. The other is based completely on personal conviction. Is there a problem with believing merely on the basis of authority? No, as long as the authority is correct. But what if the authority is wrong? Who will be to blame if you trust an authority that was in error? Admittedly, the authority is somewhat to blame, but for the most part you are to blame for believing them. Let's look at a frightening example. What if you die and wake up to find that God is actually not a Trinity, but an alligator-looking creature named Mr. Bulbous. He mocks you for believing in Jesus and forces you into slave labor. Take a minute to think of whom you would blame for your fate. If you thought of anyone other than yourself, you have to wonder if you have truly made your faith your own. Once you have reached the point that you can say that you are solely responsible for your faith, then you can say that the faith is truly yours.

Unfortunately, a belief with mere authority as its foundation is more likely to be renounced. If a believer is confronted by an issue that contradicts his faith, he has the choice to abandon that faith or resolve that issue. The issue may not be merely intellectual. The believer may be considering going out drinking with his roommates, or a young Christian girl may be struggling with the physical nature of her relationship with her boyfriend.

A young man may be hindered by his science teacher's naturalist remarks, or possibly a woman begins to experiment with the new age movement with the help of some Wiccan friends. No matter, every Christian will someday come to a crossroad and will have to decide which way to go. It is true that this may not be one single choice; it may be multiple choices made over a number of years. Nonetheless, the crossroads lie ahead and the decisions will directly affect your faith and your personal walk with God. If your faith is based merely on the authority of another, then you have a good chance of making a bad decision, a decision that may have devastating effects on your faith.

Preparing for a Crossroad

I went to a private Christian college and during my freshman year I was placed in an Introduction to Philosophy class that was taught by a brilliant Christian professor. Without a doubt it was the most intellectually challenging class I had ever taken. The professor probably had no idea of the effect that every session had on my psyche. I always left wondering about the issues that were discussed. It was over the course of this semester that I found myself at a crossroad. I had been confronted by many questions I was afraid to ask and doubts that remained unanswered.

Being at a crossroad is never pleasant. Another description of a crossroad is a "crisis of belief." It is called a crisis for a good reason. If you could take everything you believed and mold it into a ball and fling that ball into outer space, then you would have the feelings encountered while in a crisis of belief. You simply question everything you believe to be true. Is God real? Is the world real? Could it be that my parents, pastors, and friends are all wrong?

The following are three lessons that I learned during my crisis of belief:

1) They could be wrong. It seems as though there may need to be a disclaimer on this issue: let it be known that the author of this book is a Christian and I believe that Christianity is true in every sense of the word. Yet, it also did me well to realize that there are literally billions of people who do not believe in the gospel of Jesus Christ. At current estimates there are over a billion Muslims and almost a billion Hindus in the world. The point to be made here is that there are many, many people in the world that do not believe that Christ is the way to salvation.

I realized that there is a large quantity of people who really believe that the doctrines of Islam, Buddhism, or whatever religion they subscribe to, are REAL. They teach their children that their religious beliefs are grounded in REALITY. Since only one of these religions could be correct, then there are billions of parents, religious leaders, and scholars who are teaching their children and their nations a falsehood.

I had to come to grips with the fact that since billions of other parents are wrong, it was possible that my parents could also be wrong. It may seem to you that this is not that difficult of a task. There are often times when children disagree with their parents. Yet it seems that when the issue revolves around your view of reality and your view of the supernatural, it is much tougher to disagree with your parents. For instance, I once taught an Old Testament class for eighth grade students. At one point during a lesson, the topic turned to the attributes and abilities of God. A student insisted that God could do anything He wanted, while I contended that God could do anything that was perfect; I denied that God could do anything evil. I gave the examples that God cannot lie, sin, or die. Yet a few of the students wouldn't hear anything of it! Why? Because their parents had taught them from their childhood that God could do ANYTHING.

The principle I learned was simply this; because it is possible that my parents were genuine and sincere people, but people who might be wrong, I could not believe in the tenets of Christianity based solely on the authority of my parents. I needed to develop my own faith, my own reason for believing, so that the Christian faith could be my faith and not merely the faith of my parents.

2) Doubt is Unavoidable. Because of the nature of time, faith, and humanity, doubt is inescapable. As human beings we are frequently second-guessing ourselves. Whenever a decision is made, whether important or seemingly inconsequential, we can look back and wonder, "what if I had made a different choice?" It seems that the smallest choice could change a lifetime. Even one moment of suspended judgment, or yielded temptation, or fueled anger, can condemn a person for life. Because we live in a temporal world where moment follows moment, we can look back and doubt our past choices.

These choices may not be doubted because of the consequences, but also because over time the reasons why we first believed may not seem as effective as they first appeared. You may have placed faith in a person for specific reasons, and later those reasons seem unable to convince you that you should continue to trust this person. It seems that this issue is the cause of many cases of "crisis of belief." For whether your faith in Christ is based on the authority of your parents, the feelings associated with the times spent with Christ in prayer and the Holy Spirit in worship, or strong intellectual reasons, no matter, each of these can be doubted. Over time you can come to believe that your parents might be wrong about their faith. The feelings associated with being present with God can be long forgotten after some time has passed. At some point a friendly atheist may critique your theistic arguments, leaving you feeling like the intellectual reasons you once grasped are now less than adequate. No matter what the basis of your faith is, or if it is a combination of all of these, they each in their own way can deteriorate. Because of the nature of time and the changes that may happen over a succession of moments, our faith may become infected with doubt.

We must also consider the nature of faith itself to adequately argue this point. The clearest definition of perfect faith is found in Hebrews 11:1, "Now faith is the substance of things hoped for, the evidence of things not seen." There are a few points here in this definition that need to be clarified for our study of the nature of faith to continue.

First, it must also be stated that there is a drastic difference between knowledge (or reason) and faith. For one can explain God's existence to a friend in such an eloquent way that by the end of the conversation the friend KNOWS that God exists. But there is a drastic difference between knowing that God exists and trusting in Him. It seems that these two concepts become very confused by Christians and the public at large. Most Americans would claim to be Christian, but what do they mean by "Christian"? Some of them may have gone to Sunday school as children and are able to name a few books of the Bible. Others may believe that God exists and that Jesus is his son, but do either of these facts make the person a Christian? It seems that this mere knowledge about Christianity is not adequate for salvation. There needs to be a trust in Christ for daily needs and for eternal salvation; and for this trust to exist, there must be some sort of relationship between the person and God. This trust is what we mean when we use the term "faith."

Thomas Aquinas, a medieval philosopher, distinguished faith and reason in this way: "The mind of the one believing settles upon the one side of a question not in virtue of his reason but in virtue of his will. Therefore assent is understood in the definition [of faith] as an act of the mind in so far as the mind is brought to its decision by the will."[9] Thus Aquinas asserted that reason could not force faith. Faith inherently involves a choice by the individual and while reason may be involved in the choice, it cannot force the choice.

---

[9] Thomas Aquinas, *De Trinitate*, 2a2ae. 2, 1, ad 3.

Secondly, faith does not utilize science to find its basis. In science there is a principle called **perfect induction**. This applies to situations where the results of a hypothesis are easily proven by simple investigation. For example, "There are two coins in my pocket." To find the answer, I would simply pull out my pocket and thus the hypothesis would easily be proven true or false. This type of hypothesis testing is not applicable to faith. A believer in God cannot go out and "find him" to show to a non-believing neighbor. It should be strongly argued that this does not mean that there is no evidence in the realm of faith. It simply means that perfect induction has no role in faith.

Third, we may argue philosophically, or even use forensic science to give proof that God exists. Yet these arguments cannot force a person to have faith that God exists. The listener must choose to believe that he exists. Even more so, in the case of Christ, it is impossible to prove scientifically that Christ is who he said he is. There are no experiments to conduct that would 100% prove that Jesus is God. The statements of Christ could be supported by philosophical and historical evidence, but this cannot prove that he must be God. The faithless must choose faith in order to have faith.

The point is that having faith is not easy. Paul makes this apparent when he points out that the object of our faith is not *directly* observable.[10] The fact of the matter is that it is difficult to be certain of something that we don't see. Jesus readily condemned those who were close to him who lacked faith, for these men saw his work with their own eyes. Many pulpits have been witness to the story of Thomas and his doubts in the risen Christ. But what is most inspirational is what Jesus said immediately after this incident: "Because you have seen me, you have believed; blessed are those who have not seen and yet have believed."[11]

Having a lack of faith is bound to happen. If there were a formula to keep the reader from ever encountering doubt, it would have already been distributed. But because of the nature of humanity and our environment, doubt is unavoidable; but that does not mean that we should be complacent when doubt arises. The most important thing is to find the proper way to react when doubt rears its ugly head.

Doubt is inherently a lack of certainty concerning one's faith, so in some sense it should be viewed as a privation of something perfect. It is

---

[10] The word "directly" is emphasized due to the fact that theists believe that God is *indirectly* visible through his effects. *See Cosmological Argument.*
[11] John 20:29.

God's wish that we should be perfect, as Jesus himself said in Matthew 5:48, "Be perfect, therefore, as your heavenly Father is perfect." If we doubt, we should attempt to eliminate that doubt and strive for perfect faith. Regrettably, it seems that some religious authorities want to simply squelch doubt rather than to deal with the issue. I have a Jewish friend who, while in college, went back to his hometown with some questions for his rabbi. The rabbi was not willing to answer any question dealing with the possibility that Jesus was the messiah. The young Jew went back to college with none of his questions answered and with his faith in jeopardy. By the grace of God, that young Jew sought truth. This resulted in him finding Christ, and eventually a professorship at an evangelical seminary.

It seems that when doubts arise, the correct thing to do is not to squelch them inside, or pretend that they don't exist, but rather, seek the truth. Peter Abelard, the twelfth century theologian wrote, "By doubting we come to examine and by examining we reach the truth."[12] If Christianity is true, and you honestly seek the truth, the result of your endeavors will be a stronger faith in Christ. The only problem is that many of us do not have the time or fortitude to investigate our doubts. Additionally, it seems that some Christians act as if doubt is an unforgivable sin; so many young people hold these doubts inside and pretend that their faith is strong. Unfortunately, it may be the ignoring of doubt that is the more severe problem. James informs us in James 4:17, "Anyone, then, who knows the good he ought to do and doesn't do it, sins." Thus, in knowing that a doubt is a lack of perfection, and God calls us to strive toward perfection, we should do all that we can to seek truth and eliminate doubt. If help is needed along the way, ask a trusted friend, teacher, or pastor for help. If a friend asks you for help, be open and honest, and work to help your friend through that trying time. Doubt is a burden that should be shared among Christians, not disregarded and ignored. Face doubt and conquer it!

3) Faith is essential yet Reason should be utilized. One day my philosophy professor was being questioned by the students about his own faith. It seemed as though one specific student was really hammering him with questions. I couldn't tell if the student really wanted to know the answers or was simply badgering the professor into submission. No matter the case, this final question was asked of the professor while he was erasing the blackboard, "How do you really know for sure that Christianity is real?" As the question was asked the professor slammed his eraser to the wall and

[12] Peter Abelard, *Sic et Non*, edited by Blanche Boyer and Richard McKeon (Chicago: University of Chicago Press, 1977), 1120.

with his back still turned to the class he said with a strong but passionate voice, "I've bet my life on it."

Let it be known that betting on something with all of your body and soul will not make something real. A gambler could put all of his money on the sad hopes that a horse will finish a race ahead of the others, but his dedication to the horse will not affect the outcome of the race. My professor's point was not that you merely needed to have faith in order to decide what is real, but he later explained that he had chosen what was real by using a combination of reason and faith to determine reality. Even beyond that, he realized that the choice he made for Christianity was no mere choice, but one on which his life and his afterlife depended. He literally had "bet his life" that Christianity was real.

For some this is a difficult topic, but once it is realized that most people utilize faith and reason in almost every decision in life, it will become obvious that accepting Christianity is no different. For the first example, let's examine the decision to purchase an expensive yet essential item. You may pick the item; it may be a car or a computer or a dress to wear to the school dance. No matter, it simply needs to be an expensive yet a necessary item. Of course, you will want to utilize reason to examine all options. In every case, you want to find the best options at the best price. The item needs to fulfill as many wants and needs that you have. Yet at the same time, you must also take into account the maker of the item. No matter the item purchased, you must take into account the faith, or trust, that you have in the seller and the manufacturer of the product. You must ask yourself these questions: "Should I buy a Ford or Chevy automobile? Should I buy a Dell or a Compaq computer? Should I buy a dress made by Versace or one made by my mother?" This issue is not a minor one. For you trust that the manufacturer will not make an item of poor quality. If they break this trust you could be driving a lemon of a car, or using a computer that continually crashes, or wearing a dress that unravels at the school dance. Your decision will be based on the reasonable considerations of options and price, as well as the status of the faith that you have in the manufacturer.

If every other decision in our lives is determined by our reasonable faculties along with faith, why should our decision concerning Christianity be any different? Both of these principles seem to be essential to our discovery of what is real. To further prove this point, we should investigate what happens when reality is determined solely by faith and solely by reason.

If you believe only on faith, and you find no place for reason in your religious endeavors, you have fallen into the pit of **fideism**. Most fideists call to Hebrews 11:6 for support, "And without faith it is impossible to please God, because anyone who comes to him must believe that he exists and that he rewards those who earnestly seek him." Of course, no Christian would deny this fact. Remember, we are not arguing here about what is needed for salvation, but rather, what is REAL. You could believe that Christianity is real on the basis of faith alone, but if this is the case you have left yourself open to attacks from other religions and worldviews, while at the same time you are not able to articulate the reason for accepting your view of reality. Remember Peter's call in 1 Peter 3:15, "Always be prepared to give an answer to anyone who asks you to give the reason for the hope that you have. But do this with gentleness and respect." As Christians we are called to be willing and able to explain the reason why we believe what we believe.

Again, you do not need reason to have faith in Christ, but doesn't it seem important that the object of your faith should be real? For instance, let's say that you are in the market for an automobile, and you happened to meet a car salesman at a coffee shop. The salesman describes an amazing new car that was manufactured by a brand new company. You decide to trust him at his word and have faith that this company made a dependable car. After the discussion, the man leaves the coffee shop and you are left pondering the new car. You look at a TV in the shop and the man's picture pops on the screen. The broadcaster explains that the man had escaped an insane asylum and believes that he is a marketer for a fictitious car company. You had faith in a company that didn't even exist! Your faith was still real, but the object of that faith didn't exist.

There are those in the history of Christendom that argued that because of man's fall into sin, reason was utterly tainted to the point that it should not be trusted. While it is true that reason is fallible and that it was marred at the fall, it cannot be asserted that it was completely destroyed. For if man's reason was completely annihilated, man would now be animal, unable to think rationally. I once jokingly asked a fideist a simple mathematical question. After answering correctly, I then asked why we couldn't use the same sort of reasoning process to attempt to prove the existence of God and the reality of Christianity. While he explained, I found it ironic that he was attempting to use reason to prove that reason should not be used. It is undeniable that reason is essential to finding reality and determining which religion is real.

On the other hand, it should be stressed that reason will not save you. The statement above is easily recognized, for the Bible is filled with references to salvation by faith. It was said most notably by Paul in Romans

3:22, "The righteousness from God comes through faith in Jesus Christ to all who believe." Also, in Ephesians 2:8 Paul reveals, "For it is by grace you have been saved, through faith- and this is not from yourselves, it is the gift of God." Faith is not a product of human effort. We cannot reason ourselves to faith in Christ. Faith is a gift from God. Without God's intervening hand, faith is not produced. There is no doubt that faith, not reason, is the essential ingredient for salvation.

Lastly, it should be pointed out that reason alone cannot demonstrate what is real. Faith must always be present for a decision to be made. The best example of the inescapability of faith is that you must have faith in your senses in order to determine whether what you are seeing, hearing, smelling, touching, or tasting is in fact real! It seems that reason is dependent on faith, to the point that if you don't have the initial faith in your senses you are then trapped in skepticism. For if you don't trust in your senses, how could you know anything for sure? This problem of sensory perception will be discussed in further detail in our chapter on epistemology.

Summary

Metaphysics may seem like an unusual subject for an apologetics book, but when one realizes the importance of discovering what is real, the critical nature of this type of study becomes clear. Discovering what is real should affect our lifestyle, our behavior, our life, and our afterlife. In all honesty, if it is discovered that Jesus isn't real, or that he never existed, then the Christian should jump ship and never swim back![13] But the fact of the matter is that Jesus was and IS real. He really exists and sits at the right hand of the Father. If a Christian truly grasps that fact and lives day by day with that truth in mind, his walk with Christ will be an amazing one.

Nevertheless, we will all hit crossroads where our belief is attacked by doubt and our walk with Christ may become bumpy. The use of reason during these times to support our faith is critical for a Christian's faith to become re-stabilized. Yet the Christian must take the time to seek the truth and find out the answers to their lingering questions. The choice is up to you: should you ignore the doubt and let it be a stumbling block to your relationship with God, or should you bravely seek the truth?

Study Questions

1. Compare and contrast metaphysics and physics.

---

[13] 1 Cor. 15:12.

2. On what basis have you justified your belief? Do you believe based essentially on faith, the authority of another, or do you have other reasons for believing? If so, what are the reasons?
3. What is the difference between saving faith and knowledge (or reason)? Asked in another way: what is the difference between knowing God exists and trusting in him?
4. When does doubting God become a bad thing? What should you do when doubts arise? What should you do when a friend confides in you that they have doubts?
5. Have you ever hit a major crossroads in your life? If so, could you explain? If not, are you worried about possible crossroads in the future?
6. Do you believe that in some way doubt can be a good thing? Give an example.

Terms to Consider

Metaphysics
Maya
Metaphysical Realism
Idealism
Principle of uniformity
Fideism
Perfect Induction

Memory Verse Options

Hebrews 11:1 (NKJV)
Matthew 5:48 (NIV)
John 20:29 (NIV)

Going Beyond the Call of Duty: Readings for the Overachiever

College students:

Aquinas, Thomas. *Being and Essence.* Translated by Peter King. Indianapolis: Hackett Publishing, 2005.

———. *Commentary on Aristotle's Metaphysics.* Translated by John Rowan. Notre Dame: Dumb Ox Books, 1965.

Aristotle. *Metaphysics.* Vol. 8, in *Great Books of the Western World,* ed. Robert Maynard Hutchins. Chicago: Encyclopedia Britannica, 1952.

Owens, Joseph. *An Elementary Christian Metaphysics*. Milwaukee: Bruce Publishing Company, 1963. Reprint, Houston: Center for Thomistic Studies, 1986.

High School students:

Kreeft, Peter. *Summa of the Summa: The Essential Philosophical Passages of St. Thomas Aquinas' Summa Theologica Edited and Explained for Beginners.* Ft. Collins: Ignatius Press, 1990.

"I am the Way
the Truth
and the Life."

Chapter 3

What Is Truth?

"I am the way, the truth, and the life." [1]
—Jesus Christ

What Does It Mean for Something to be Called "Truth"?

THE QUESTION of truth is similar to the metaphysical question discussed in the last chapter due to the fact that both are age-old problems that have many proposed solutions. Even the ancient philosophers asked such questions: Is there such a thing as absolute truth? How do we know whether a statement is true or false? How do we determine what is true? Most readers of this text can probably posit their own common sense answer to this question. If this topic were discussed in a class setting, the majority of you would likely conclude with the same answer. In the same way that your common sense view of reality ended with realism, so will your common sense view of truth result in the correct theory.

Due to the fact that you are probably a Christian, you likely agree with the notion that God is good and that he has given humans common sense in order to make basic, educated judgments. These judgments are not intense, critical decisions, but rather, are ordinary and commonplace ones. For example, calling the hospital in an emergency and using an umbrella while walking in the rain are illustrations of common sense. In the same vein, if a person asks you if a statement is true, you will determine this by deciding if the statement is "the way it is," or if it is not "the way it is." For example, if someone states that it is raining outside, what do you do? You simply open the window to see if that is "the way it is." If it is so, the statement is true, if not, it is false. This view is the most widely held theory concerning truth and is named **the correspondence theory of**

[1] John 14:6.

31

truth. This theory denotes that if a statement corresponds to reality then it is considered to be truth.

Again, we must remember that while most people hold to this theory, there are quite a few who disagree. Therefore, we must examine all of the other theories and consider their benefits and logical inconsistencies.

The Bible and Truth

One of the most famous Biblical discussions on this subject is short, but very significant. In John's gospel, Pilate considered the question of truth while questioning Jesus. Jesus stated "'for this reason I was born, and for this I came into the world, to testify to the truth. Everyone on the side of truth listens to me.' 'What is truth?' Pilate asked. With this he went out again to the Jews and said, 'I find no basis for a charge against him.'"[2]

What seems to stand out in this quote is not anything specific that was said, but rather, what is obviously missing. Jesus never responded to Pilate's question, or at least John did not record Jesus' response. In most movies or passion plays when this passage is performed, Pilate usually asks Jesus the question on his way out of the room, usually with a scowl on his face. It is generally interpreted that Pilate wasn't really seeking an answer to the question, but was merely "having the last word" in his discussion with Jesus. No matter Pilate's motivation, Jesus could have offered him that truth if he was willing to listen with open and honest ears.

Some authors and pastors claim that Jesus is truth. Recently I heard one of my pastors claim that "truth is a person." This statement is based on John 14:6 in which Jesus stated that he was "the way and the truth and the life. No one comes to the Father except through me." This is mentioned merely to clear up some confusion and to help prevent further misunderstanding. Truth, in the normal sense of the word, is not a person; it is a property of sentences. For instance, if a person states "I am a human" and they truly are human, then the sentence is deemed true. If truth really was a person, we could claim that the true statement "I am a human" also has the property of being Jesus Christ.

All absurdity aside, the authors and pastors are simply positing that Jesus is the ultimate spiritual reality. His birth, life, death, resurrection, and glorification are all real. All of reality is founded on his blueprint, his creation, his plan, and his sustaining power. The totality of reality and all truth reduce to God.[3] In this sense, Jesus is truth. Yet be warned, when

---

[2] John 18:37–38.

[3] See Col. 1:17.

the subject of truth is discussed in the public arena, this sense of truth will not be discussed. In fact, the case in John 14:6 is the only place where Jesus called himself truth. Generally, he used the term in the normal sense. Many times Jesus began his discourses with the words, "I tell you the truth . . ." By this introduction, Jesus contended that what followed was real and that his statements corresponded to reality.

The Four Theories of Truth

① *The Pragmatic Theory of Truth*

Examination—The pragmatic view of truth is the concept that truth is not determined by a simple observation of reality, but rather by the results of a given proposition or set of propositions. The theory in simplified terms is: *whatever works, is true*. If a statement is useful and good, then the statement is true. William James, who many consider to be the father of pragmatism, wrote in his article "Pragmatism's Conception of Truth," "You can say of [a statement] either that 'it is useful because it is true' or that 'it is true because it is useful.' Both these phrases mean exactly the same thing, namely here is an idea that gets fulfilled and can be verified."[4] Thus the truth of the statement is not determined by reality, but rather by the usefulness of the results. The individual makes the statement true by his determination that it is 'useful.' William James concludes, "The truth of an idea is not a stagnant property inherent in it. Truth happens to an idea. It becomes true, is made true by events."[5]

Critique—It must be mentioned that the pragmatic view of truth has some validity when one is considering practical decisions. For instance, if you have two options to get to school: take the bus or ride with a friend, one of them may be the better choice. The actual proposition would read: It is better for me to _____ to get to school. Before the decision is made, you mentally place both options in the blank and decide which to do. Of course, you may not know which is true until both options are tested. So for a week you would ride the bus, then the next week you would ride with a friend. After those two weeks you could determine which of the options produce the best way for you to get to school in a safe and timely manner.

---

[4] William James, "Pragmatism's Conception of Truth," in *Essays in Pragmatism* (Hafner Press: New York, 1948), 162.

[5] Ibid., 161.

While pragmatism seems to work in practical decision-making, it does not work anywhere else. One of the biggest problems in this system is that the definition of what is "good and useful" is never explained. James, in his "What Pragmatism Means" writes, "The true is the name of whatever proves itself to be good in the way of belief, and good, too, for definite, assignable reasons."[6] Yet who decides what is good? It seems that "good" could be different for everybody. The pragmatic view of truth then reduces to relativism: what can be true, or good, for you may not be true, or good, for another.

Simply speaking, just because something works doesn't make it true. For instance, take a perjurer in a court of law. A person may lie on the witness stand in order to prevent the conviction of a friend, but this lie is definitely not the truth! The lie "worked" and was "useful," but was not truthful. For another example, consider a student who turns in a paper that was written by a different student. It may work for him and be very useful, but plagiarism is not truthful.

Another fatal flaw with this theory is that William James confused cause and effect. Simply speaking, he asserted that the proof for truth, or the effect, was more important than the truth itself. Something isn't true because it works, but rather, something works because it is true. Consider an electrician who has some electrical problems in his kitchen. He decides to rewire the entire room. After his job is complete he walks to the breaker switch to turn the power on in the kitchen. He knows that if he made a wiring error the breaker would kick off and he would have to solve the problem. He turns on the breaker. The lights and appliances come back on with no problem. The question is this: Was his wiring "true" before he turned the breaker back on? The answer is YES. He simply proved it to be true when he discovered that the system worked properly. The electrical system worked because his wiring was true; it wasn't true because it worked.

The pragmatic view can be used to test in order to see if a statement is FALSE, but it is not a good theory to determine truth. For instance, a man comes to town selling medicine to heal any medical condition. You took the medicine but it did not cure your athlete's foot. It didn't work. You now know that his words were not true. Thus you can use the pragmatic theory to prove something false, but not true.

Lastly, it seems that the pragmatic view of truth may be self-defeating. For if the pragmatic view of truth states "that which works is true,"

[6] William James, "What Pragmatism Means," in *Essays in Pragmatism* (Hafner Press: New York, 1948), 155.

and the pragmatic view of truth does not work, then it is not true. If the theory is useless, then why should we believe it?

The uselessness of this theory comes down to the ability to forecast the results. In the example used above, the student had to choose between taking the bus to school or riding with a friend. Let us suppose that the student decided that taking the bus was the best method. A week later, the bus is struck by a drunk driver and the student becomes injured. It was unforeseeable that this accident would happen. There was no evidence that this wreck would take place. The bus driver had a clean record and the bus was in new condition. The accident was just that, an accident. In light of the pragmatic view of truth, it is unforeseeable to be sure of the effects, thus it is unforeseeable to be sure of the truth. If we cannot be certain of truth, we are left in the pit of skepticism. Since the goal of the pragmatic approach is to find truth, yet it ultimately leaves us in skepticism, it then seems that the theory doesn't work.

② *The Coherence Theory of Truth*

Examination—The coherence theory of truth states that a statement is true if the statement is consistent, or coheres, with the other statements in a system. For instance, if you were told that a mouse just ran across the floor you may be surprised by the presence of a rodent, but you still believe that it is possible that the event occurred. Yet, if you were told that a mouse literally floated across the room on a miniature magic carpet, you may be a little more doubtful. Flying mice are not a part of our "system" of sense experience. We do not come across flying mice every day. The concept does not cohere with what we know to be possibly true.

This theory is also applicable in different worldview and religious systems. For if a Christian claims that God has healed him from a horrible disease, the atheist will simply reject the statement as false. The concept of God does not fit in the atheist's system, so the idea that God healed someone is as ridiculous as a mouse flying on a magic carpet. The atheist simply rejects the possible truth of the statement because it does not cohere with the rest of his beliefs.

The coherence view of truth also trickles over into the ethical realm. The conventionalist view of morality, which will be explained in much more detail in the chapter on ethics, contends that you should judge whether something is right or wrong solely by comparing it to the social norms of your specific culture. For instance, in America it would be quite acceptable, even praiseworthy, if you were to invite a bunch of friends over to your home for a cookout. However, if you were to travel to India, where cows are considered sacred, you might be criticized and possibly ostracized by your newfound friends. The eating of cow is simply not accepted in their culture, thus it is deemed that the action is "wrong."

Critique—Initially one must wonder how the coherentist accepted his "system" in the first place. If the coherentist has a system full of propositions, how did he accept the first statement of his system? How did he declare that first statement to be true? At some point in time, he did not have a system. So how did he accept the system? There are only two options: by faith or by examining reality. He either accepted these statements on blind faith or he used the correspondence theory of truth to determine that the original statements actually corresponded to what was real. If the first option is correct, then the coherentist is deemed an anti-intellectual fideist. Yet, if he chooses the other then he must admit that his system depends on the correspondence theory of truth.

Secondly, it seems that this theory of truth completely disregards one of the foundational laws of logic. Aristotle discovered these simplistic yet foundational laws almost 400 years before the birth of Christ. In this case, the law of non-contradiction has been broken. The **law of non-contradiction** simply states that any given thing cannot be that thing and its contradiction at the same time and the same sense. For example, Shakespeare wrote in Act III Scene I of *Hamlet*, ". . . to be or not to be, that is the question" and he was right! There is no middle ground! You can't partially exist.

Everyone believes in this law, even though some say that they don't. Of course, not believing in this law is ridiculous. Avicenna, the great Medieval Muslim philosopher wrote, "Anyone who denies the law of non-contradiction should be beaten and burned until he admits that to be beaten is not the same as not to be beaten, and to be burned is not the same as not to be burned." While this is a little extreme, no one can argue against his point. In fact, if someone says, "I don't believe in the law of non-contradiction," reply, "So you do believe it!" For to say that you don't believe something is actually implying the law! If they honestly don't believe the law, they would have to argue that believing in the law and not believing in the law are identical concepts!

There are two ways that the law of non-contradiction is broken by coherentists. First, a statement could be both true and false! For instance, take the above example of the Christian who claimed to be healed. In his system the statement is true but in the atheist's it is false. The statement cannot be both true and false at the same time! They cannot both be correct. Either God healed the Christian or he didn't. At least one of the two must be wrong! Secondly, we also need to consider the systems as a whole. With two people, you could have two very coherent systems with completely opposing propositions within. Norman Geisler remarks, "It is at least logically possible to have two internally coherent systems of statements which are, however, mutually incompatible so that both cannot be true without sacrificing the law of non-contradiction. A defender of the coherence theory could reply that we should then accept the more comprehensive system as true. However, this does not alleviate the problem, because it is equally possible that these internally coherent but mutually incompatible systems could also be *equally* comprehensive."[7] Thus the person who holds to the coherence view of truth has two alternatives: violate the law of non-contradiction and say both systems are true or produce some other way of determining that one is false and the other is true. Since the role of the coherence view of truth is to find truth, and the coherentist has to find another way of determining truth, it seems as though his view of truth needs revision, or it should simply be thrown in the scrap pile.

Lastly, it also can be argued that a system of beliefs could be thoroughly coherent but wrong. For example, let's suppose that a man went on trial for the death of a neighbor. He told intricate and scrupulous lies to cover his evil ways. The lies were so detailed and seemingly correct that the jury acquits the man of any wrongdoing. The murderer has spun a web of lies to free himself, yet were his statements true? The story gelled into one intricate system, yet not one of the propositions was true. The system as a whole cohered, but the propositions did not correspond to reality.

It must be pointed out that coherence can be used to test in order to see if a statement is FALSE, but it is not a good theory to determine truth. For example, let's examine a world religion such as Islam. The Muslims believe that their holy book, the Quran, is without error. It is one of the major tenets of Islam. Just like in Christianity, their holy book is the foundation for the entire religion. Yet let's suggest that there are serious errors in the book. What if there were completely contradictory statements throughout the work? These statements would show that Islam is not a completely coherent religion, and thus it is likely untrue. So coherence could be a great TEST for truth, but not an adequate theory about the nature of truth.

---

[7] Norman Geisler and Paul D. Feinberg, *Introduction to Philosophy: A Christian Perspective* (Grand Rapids: Baker Book House, 1980), 238.

god redefines truth, there is no truth at all,

Relativism

③ *The Subjective Theory of Truth*

Examination—The subjective theory of truth is one of the most prevailing and damaging concepts that have permeated the college campus, as well as infiltrated the general secular culture. In this view of truth the individual decides what is true and false based merely on his own personal desires. In other words, the person claims truth is simply what they want to be true. If they feel like something is true, then it is true.

The subjective theory is also called relativism. It has gained this title due to the fact that it asserts that truth is relative to each individual. One person may claim that a proposition is true, while another person could claim that the same proposition is false. Instead of arguing about it, they will agree that they both are right. The following paragraph from Ernie Manning will illustrate this point. The writer simply does not want to offend anyone, and is unwilling to claim that there is an ultimate and absolute truth:

> God's greatest strength is that through all things he shines clear and true. Every person on this planet is witness to and of his creation. It is no coincidence that the world has many different religious beliefs and denominations. Which one is right is not a question that deserves an answer because it defeats God's purpose. God wants to teach us all one thing and is not bound by one denomination or belief system. God inspires people in different ways and so different people will speak of him differently. For example, I don't expect a Buddhist to accept and embrace Christianity, or vice versa. They both have similar practices and at the core do encourage devotion to a higher deity. For me to say that you shouldn't believe one thing or the other is too easy to bring reference to being judgmental.[8]

Critique—The question that needs to be asked to the writer of the above paragraph is simple: is there an actual supernatural deity and if so, who is he? Is there truly a deity that exists? If so, there are only three possibilities:

1. The supernatural deity is one of the supernatural beings expressed in one of the modern world religions.
2. God exists, but he is not expressed in any world religion.
3. The deity is a mixture of all these different deities that are expressed in all of these various religions.

[8] Ernie Manning, Internet, http://www.geocities.com/coolpoete/lion_of_judah.htm, June 2004.

If the relativist takes the first notion and argues that the supernatural being is one specific deity, then he cannot be a relativist. For a relativist must argue that truth depends on the person. So the theology of the Buddhist, Hindu, Muslim, Jew, and the Christian are all correct! Thus the relativist cannot claim that any one religion is more or less true than another.

The relativist could not hold the second option due to the fact that he would be telling every religious person in the world that his religion was wrong. If a relativist states that "none of the world religions have the true god" then he has made an absolute statement. As a proper relativist, you cannot make a claim that is absolutely true for everyone. If this sort of statement is made by the relativist, he is not a true relativist, but a masquerading absolutist.

The relativist's last option is that god is a blend of all of the different deities of all the various religions. This category of relativism is called pluralism. The word pluralism is used to denote that a plurality of contradictory ideas about God are all correct. Your first query to the relativist should be, "How would this be possible?" For if a Native American Indian claimed that the sun was his god and I claimed that God is spirit[9], it would seem that both of these statements could not be true. Again, if I claim that God is a Trinity and a Hindu claims that his god is named Ganesh and has an elephant head, then at least one of us must be wrong!

Let's look at a more practical example. If you meet a friend who asks you, "Do you know Jeff?" you immediately begin to think of all the different people that you know who are named Jeff. Then you begin to sift through them and consider which is the Jeff of which they are speaking. Of course, you must consider that you do not know this specific Jeff at all! Thus you begin to ask questions such as: "What is his hair color?" and "How old is he?" If your friend mentions that he is a blonde, eighteen year old who goes to school at Jefferson and is dating a girl named Julie, and you know of a Jeff that fits that description, you would answer, "Sure, I know Jeff." You simply took what you knew of the "real Jeff" and compared it to the description. The theology of the relativist flies in the face of this example. The relativist would argue that both the Hindu deities and the Christian God are both true, and that the religions of the Muslim and the Israelite are equally correct. If there is a God, specifically the Christian God in which we believe, he must be a specific God in the same way that

[9] John 4:24.

Jeff must be a specific Jeff. He should have some absolute, concrete attributes that give him his character and differentiate him from his creation.

Relativism and Absolute Truth

The overall problem with the relativists' position is the negation of the possibility of absolute truth. Absolute truth is simply the notion that there is a truth or a set of truths that apply to everyone. To be clear, it must be realized that absolutely true statements are dependent on the person, time and location by which they are said. For instance, I could say today that "I am in North Carolina," and this statement, in its given context, is an absolute truth. You may not be able to repeat the phrase truthfully because you may not be in the same state. It must also be pointed out that in a few days I will have to say, "I am in Florida" due to the fact that I will have traveled to that state. This does not make truth relative! Truth claims are essentially bound by time, place, and author. Thus both claims are absolutely true and are dependent on the location of the author of the statements.

A second point about absolute truth is that it is not a matter of opinion. For instance, let's suppose that there is a classroom full of students in which half of them say that it is cold and the other half say it is not cold; this is not a proof of relativism. First, consider what is meant by "cold." It seems that the word itself denotes that "being cold" is an opinion and not a proposed truth about the actual temperature in the classroom. Yet secondly, one must realize that the temperature itself *is* an absolute truth. So at 8:00 PM on Friday, August 30th, it is officially 74 degrees in this classroom. There may be many opinions on the temperature, but the absolute truth is that it is 74 degrees!

The easiest example to prove the lunacy of relativism and the validity of absolute truth is the life and actions of Adolph Hitler. If someone demands that there is no such thing as absolute truth, ask him if it was acceptable for Hitler to kill millions of Jews. The relativist is left with a harsh dilemma. A true relativist would have to respond that Hitler's actions were "true for Hitler" so it must have been morally acceptable. Either the relativist abandons the concept of relativism, or they end up looking like an immoral lunatic. Who in their right mind would argue that it was acceptable for Hitler to commit such heinous genocide? If they say that genocide is wrong, they then are purporting this absolute truth: "Genocide is wrong for everyone in every culture and every location." The irony of relativism is that it is completely self-defeating. Relativism cannot even pass its own test for truth. For if someone claims that "all truth is relative" doesn't that fall under the definition of an absolute truth? Isn't the relativist suggesting that relativism truly applies to everyone in every culture and at all times and locations? Norman Geisler in the book *Why I am a Christian* writes, "What is more, feelings are relative to individuals. What feels good to one person may feel bad to another. If so, then truth would be relative. But all truth cannot be relative. The truth claim that "all truth is relative" is offered as an absolute truth."[10] The relativist insists, usually unknowingly, that relativism itself is an absolute truth! Thus, if a relativist tells you that truth is relative, simply respond with "Is that absolutely true?" Again, he is left with a dilemma. If he says that relativism is absolutely true, then he has thus rejected relativism, for relativists must insist that there is no such thing as absolute truth. Then again, if he says that relativism is not absolutely true, then he cannot argue that relativism is something that everyone must believe in.

Those who believe in the subjective view of truth simply state that if it feels right, then it is true. Yet, one can easily discover that what may "feel good" to one person may not be true. For instance, a person may find out some really horrible news such as the occurrence of a national or personal tragedy. These truths may make a person feel horrible, yet they are the truth. The facts correspond to reality! In fact, many people go through a phase of denial after tragedies because they feel so horrible that they wish to deny the truth. But the *fact of the matter* is that the event occurred and the tragedy did transpire.

⑨ *The Correspondence Theory of Truth*

The correspondence theory of truth is the most widely accepted theory of truth. For those who have never considered the different theories of truth, this theory is usually already assumed. If the discussions in this chapter are new to you, it is very likely that this is the view that you have made your own. The correspondence theory states that in order for something to be considered true, it must correspond to reality. Truth simply is "the way it is;" it is "putting reality into words." For example, if I were to point to a chair and state, "this is a chair," then that statement would be considered true. Of course, a claim to the opposite effect would be considered false. So if I then pointed to a chair and stated, "this is a _____" and did not state the word "chair," the sentence would be false. It would not matter if

[10] Norman Geisler and Paul Hoffman, *Why I am a Christian: Leading Thinkers Explain Why they Believe* (Grand Rapids: Baker Books, 2001), 33.

I put the word "moose" in the blank, or the word "table," or even a similar word like "chair-rail"; the sentence would still be false.

Notice how one's view of metaphysics, or their view of reality, is directly linked to one's view of truth. Those who are skeptical about reality and feel that it is impossible to be sure of what is real, seemingly have a problem with this view of truth. For if you cannot adequately know reality, then you cannot be sure if any given statement corresponds to reality. According to this definition of the truth, if you cannot be sure what corresponds to reality, then you cannot know truth. Likewise, an absolute idealist would have a problem finding ultimate truth. For if you are an idealist, you would argue that what is most "real" is not physical, but is rather the ideas in your mind. Unless we grasp onto the correspondence theory of truth, truth will be considered subjective and relative to each individual.

Summary

Over the preceding pages we have tackled the issue of truth. We have considered four different theories of truth: coherence, pragmatic, subjective, and correspondence. While the coherence and pragmatic views are adequate ways to test whether something is false, they are ineffective in classifying what is truth. Only the correspondence theory seems to accurately describe the nature of truth. As Christians, we need to understand that relativism is a tool of the deceiver used to make us believe that truth and reality revolve around each individual person. The only way to defeat him is to be able to understand and explain the correspondence theory of truth.

Study Questions

1. Explain how the pragmatic and coherence views of truth are merely tests for truth, or rather; discuss how these views of truth can only prove something false. Give examples to support your answers.
2. In what way is Jesus "the truth?" How is this different from what most people normally mean when they say something is "true?"
3. Define relativism and give your own example of how relativism is the wrong view of truth.
4. Use a Bible concordance to find where the Bible mentions the word "truth." Do not use John 14:6 as your example. Write down the entire verse and explain what the author meant when he used the word "truth."

5. How does a person's metaphysics relate to their view of truth? It may help to define the correspondence theory as well as the realist's view of reality.

Terms to Consider

Absolute Truth
Relativism
Pluralism
The Coherence Theory of Truth
The Pragmatic Theory of Truth
The Subjective Theory of Truth
The Correspondence Theory of Truth
Law of non-contradiction

Memory Verse Options

John 18:37 (Abridged to Jesus' words)
John 14:6

Going Beyond the Call of Duty: Readings for the Overachiever

College students:

Norman Geisler and Paul D. Feinberg. *Introduction to Philosophy: A Christian Perspective*. (Grand Rapids: Baker Book House), 1980.

High School students:

Beckwith, Francis and Gregory Koukl. *Relativism: Feet Firmly Planted in Mid-Air*. (Grand Rapids: Baker Book House), 1998.

Copan, Paul. *True for you, but not for me*. (Minneapolis: Bethany House), 1998.

Groothuis, Doug. *Truth Decay: Defending Christianity Against the Challenges of Postmodernism*. (Downers Grove: Intervarsity Press), 2000.

Chapter 4

Epistemology: How Do We Know What We Know?

"Knowledge is the manifestation and declaration of the already realized accord between intellect and being; knowledge results, and literally flows, from truth as an effect from its cause."[1]
—Etienne Gilson

What Is Knowledge?

THE FOLLOWING chapter will undertake the subject of epistemology. The word **epistemology** is simply defined as the study of knowledge. While the definition of epistemology appears uncomplicated, the actual study of knowledge is very complex. Although we all profess that to have obtained "knowledge" over the years, most of us probably haven't contemplated the nature of knowledge. Let's begin with what may appear to be a simple question: "What is Knowledge?"

It could probably be assumed that most of the readers of this book have not considered the definition of the word "knowledge." Isn't it ironic that young people can go through thirteen or more years of education and still not be given the meaning of this all-important term? Teachers seem to be so proud that they have dispensed knowledge to their students, yet usually neither the teacher nor the student can define what the word means. So, what then is the definition of knowledge? What does it mean to "know" something? To say that knowledge is simply "ideas" seems too vague and to use the term "facts" to define knowledge appears incomplete. How should we explain such a complex concept?

The three-word definition of **knowledge** is simply *Justified True Belief*. To put the definition in a more understandable sentence structure it has

[1] Etienne Gilson, *The Spirit of Medieval Philosophy* (London: Sheed & Ward, 1936), chapter 12.

45

been formulated: *Knowledge describes a belief that corresponds to reality and has the justification to adequately prove it.* In order to fully comprehend the definition, the three-word definition will be broken down and clarified according to each word, beginning with the last and ending with the first.

Belief—A belief is simply something that someone claims is true. What is believed depends on each person. We all have different beliefs about various things: politics, religion, morals, and even our favorite flavor of ice cream. Some of these views are trivial and opinionated; others deal with more serious ideas and consider the state of the world and the supernatural. No matter if they are important or insignificant, all of these are beliefs, and our minds are full of them.

True—A belief must be true in order for it to be considered knowledge. If a belief does not correspond to reality, then it is not knowledge. For example, if I claim, "The world is flat," I am claiming a falsehood and it is not knowledge. Imagine that you overhear a conversation between two people who are arguing about something that happened the night before. One of the debaters claims, "I *know* that this is what happened." By stressing the "know," they are suggesting that they have knowledge and that their statements are true. Whether you realize it or not, the word "knowledge" implies the concept of truth.

As a brief note, it should be mentioned that in some sense, we could have knowledge *about* an untruth. For instance if I say, "Muslims believe that Jesus is not God," then this is a true statement and is thus knowledge. This is a true statement *about* a false religion that contains an incorrect statement about Jesus Christ. Now if I say, "Jesus is not God," then I have stated a falsehood and it is not knowledge.

Justified—One may ask, "Well then what about all of these other ideas popping around my brain? I am unsure if they are true, so are they still knowledge?" Well, these are simply ideas and beliefs and not knowledge. For an idea must have some justification in order to be considered knowledge. The concept of justification is of extreme importance in this chapter; for your understanding of how something is justified will determine your understanding of what can be categorized as "knowledge."

Before we dive into examples of justification, it should be acknowledged that there would rarely be a time when one can justify a claim to a degree of 100%. As mentioned in chapter 2, unless something is a perfect induction, you cannot prove it 100%. If you have not noticed before, you will begin to become very acquainted with those that state that unless something is justified to perfection, then they will not believe it. Unfortunately, these are the same folks who have problems believing in

God. As we have discussed earlier, there is almost always a hint of faith in every belief claim. If it were the case that we must prove something to 100% in order to be believed, then we would have a very limited view of knowledge. This sort of quasi-intellectual environment would not allow the possibility of knowledge concerning God, science, history, religion, or any faith whatsoever. Historians would be hard pressed to find 100% proof for most historical accounts, and even more so, the evolutionist would never get off the ground without plenty of faith in Darwin's theories.

It is without question that you will have some beliefs that seem to have more justification than others. This point raises an important question: how much justification is needed in order to call a belief "knowledge?" In order to understand this question, we must first realize that different claims require different types of justification. For example, let's take two truth claims: "That is my car" and "That is my mom." If a student tells me he has a new car and he points to a brand new Porsche in the parking lot, I may be a little skeptical. How could he prove this to me? He could show me his registration, his purchase order from the car company; he could quote the mileage, and even jump in and start it up with his keys. This would satisfy my skepticism and thus I would likely believe him. Yet take the second claim: "That is my mom." If the same student made this claim, would I use the same justification in order to prove that the woman he pointed to was actually his mother? I don't think it would be proper to ask for his mom's registration or purchase order, and it definitely would not be appropriate to poke her with keys and ask for her mileage. This is a silly analogy, yet it shows the simple point: for different truth claims you need to have different justifications.

With this truth in mind, you can see how it would be difficult to offer an exact answer to the question: "How much justification is needed in order to call a belief knowledge?" The question simply depends on the situation in which the people find themselves. *If a person in any given situation has exhausted all possible reasonable explanations, then the statement should be deemed knowledge.*

How Do I Justify a Belief?

One of the most important questions which is asked in this chapter is, "What type of justification is needed to show that a belief is actually 'knowledge.'" How can I tell if claims such as: "Two plus two is four," "Chester Arthur was president of the United States from 1881 to 1885," and "I have a headache," are knowledge or are falsehood? As mentioned before, how you justify a proposition will depend on the situation, but it seems that there are four prevalent types of justification: Authority, Rationality, Empiricism, and Immediate Sensory Awareness.

Most of the time, what a person may call knowledge can only be justified by sentences like: "I saw it on the news" or "My mom told me that this was true" or even worse "I saw it on the internet." This is simply justifying truth by **authority**. While this type of justification is usually problematic, it is not always bad. For example, if I have a question about physics, I will talk to an expert physicist. They are authorities on the matter. This is what happens in court cases. The lawyer will find an expert witness who gives his expert opinion. In these sorts of cases, authority may be used for justification.

Critique—Simply put, an authority can be wrong. How do we know that the authority is correct? Thus, an appeal to authority often ends in skepticism. Additionally, what happens when it comes to religious faith? Who is an expert on God? As was discussed in chapter two, most young people believe in the Christian faith simply due to the fact that they were told as children that Christianity was true. Eventually, the authority of the parents becomes questioned and the faith of the young person falters. When this happens, these three other justifications need to become utilized.

Rationality is simply the use of pure deductive logic to justify a statement. A deductive argument can be demonstrated with a simple **syllogism**[2]:

1. All men are mortal.
2. Socrates is a man.
3. Thus, Socrates is mortal

If the content of the above premises correspond to reality then the syllogism is correct and the conclusion is irrefutable. So, if all men ARE mortal, and Socrates IS a man, then Socrates MUST BE mortal.

Notice that there is no investigation involved in Rationalism. No one set out to find if it were true that Socrates was truly a man, a figment of imagination, or maybe even a dog. No person investigated the content of the syllogism. In Rationalism, the mind is given the spotlight while the senses take a back seat. Arguments of this type are usually called **a priori** arguments. Using the root of the word, we can deduce that an *a priori*

---

[2] *Syllogism*—A term in logic denoting a series of at least two premises that end in a conclusion. Deductive logic is more focused on the form of the logical argument than proving the content of the premises. Yet if the content of any premise is proven wrong, then the syllogism's conclusion is unfounded and the argument fails.

argument uses a line of reasoning *prior to* an individual using his senses for information.

The only information used in a purely rational argument is that which can be deduced logically, mathematically, or is already self evident to the individual. For instance, it would be self evident to most that all men die, thus they are mortal. Also, it would make sense to the audience of Plato, who first heard the above syllogism, that Socrates was a man. The above statements did not need to be investigated; they were already believed by the listeners.

Usually, purely rational arguments use **analytic statements** for their foundation. An analytic statement is merely a claim which includes a part of the definition of the words used in the statement. For example, "A triangle has three sides," and "A monkey is a mammal," are both analytical statements. It is a part of the definition of triangle to have three sides. If it did not have three sides, it would not be a triangle!

At first it may seem that purely rational arguments are rarely used by common individuals, but in reality, we use them every day. As an example of purely rational arguments in everyday usage, take for example this situation. If a young lady named Betty is introduced to Fred at a party and later her friend says, "Fred is Springfield's most eligible bachelor." Betty knows the implication that her friend is making: Fred is unmarried. Here is the situation in logical form:

1. All bachelors are unmarried men.
2. Fred is a bachelor.
3. Thus, Fred is an unmarried man.

Of course, Betty never considered this logical syllogism, at least, not in the three-step form above. Yet it should be realized that anytime you deduce a conclusion without investigation, you are likely using a purely rational argument.

Criticism of Rationality—Rationality is attractive because its purely rational arguments lead to logical, definite conclusions. Even though there are reasons to hold on to such a belief, there are two main problems with this form of justification. First, the question must be asked how this form of logic is based in reality. If the premises are not investigated in reality, how can we be sure that the argument is correct? The Rationalist would reply that each argument must have a universal starting point in order for the argument to hold any water. Along those lines, the second problem is revealed. But how can we be sure that the first premise is a universal starting point? Can we investigate it? No.

As an illustration, take the philosophy of the seventeenth century French idealist and rationalist: Rene Descartes. Descartes wished to use pure logic as the foundation of his entire philosophical system. Yet, since rationalists focus on logic and refuse to use their senses, of what could Descartes be sure? Could he be sure that the external world exists? Could he even justify that the chair he sat upon was real? No! He couldn't use his senses. So what could he know? He knew that he could not be sure of the external world; he doubted that it existed. But to doubt is to think, therefore his famous dictum arose: "I think therefore I am." He was sure that he existed, based solely on the fact that he was sure of his own thoughts. You can see the problem here with Descartes' system. Why would one doubt what seems blatantly obvious to the average individual? How can you prove what is true in reality without even looking at reality? Can you give evidence of a physical phenomenon by using only ideas and totally neglecting the senses?

Empiricism is the use of the senses to justify a claim. Unlike the rationalist, the empiricist focuses his attention on sensory information and assigns pure reason a lesser role in the justification of knowledge. I am sure many have heard the claim "I have to see it to believe it," and this is the heart of empiricism. The empiricist simply claims that there must be some sensory evidence, whether it be touch, taste, smell, sight, or sound, before something should be considered justified.

If the reader has not yet noticed, the field of science can be placed under the category of empiricism. The scientist investigates the observable facts of a situation, and makes his conclusion based on this evidence. Thus we can determine that scientific investigation and empirical arguments are **a posteriori** arguments, or arguments that are made *after* using the senses.

It is fairly simple to comment on the usefulness of this type of justification. If anyone makes a truth claim, all one has to do is ask for proof. If this person is able to give a sufficient amount of observable proof, then the claim is justified. It is pretty obvious that most of us use this type of reasoning on a daily basis. Anytime you feel like you need to "see something for yourself" you are requiring empirical evidence for a justification of that belief. The illustration mentioned earlier concerning the ownership of a Porsche required empirical evidence for proof. If a proper title, registration, and the keys to the car were demonstrated, then an empiricist would state that the claim "This is my Porsche," is justified.

Criticism of Empiricism—While empiricism seems to be the easy answer, we must realize that even knowledge that seems purely derived from the senses is actually dependent on the concepts in the mind. For instance, let's take for example little Billy. Billy sees something on the horizon. He approaches that thing, does a brief examination, and realizes that it is a raccoon. How did he know of this animal called "raccoon?" He already had the concept, or the idea, of what a raccoon was before he investigated the animal. Thus, it seems that it is possible that there is in actually no such thing as "pure empiricism." Many philosophers argue that ideas are essential to gaining knowledge through the senses.

David Hume, an 18th century English philosopher and a stringent empiricist, actually argued that the experiences we have are merely bundles of sensory impressions. Hume writes, "He would not, at first, by any reasoning, be able to reach the idea of cause and effect; since the particular powers, by which all natural operations are performed, never appear to the senses; nor is it reasonable to conclude, merely because one event, in one instance, precedes another, that therefore the one is the cause, the other the effect. Their conjunction may be arbitrary and casual. There may be no reason to infer the existence of one from the appearance of the other."[3] He concluded that there was no real causal connection we could know of between reality, your senses, and your ideas. Thus, we cannot be sure of what really is real, and really is true. David Hume is the most infamous skeptic who ever lived. He even concluded that it was impossible to truly know yourself!

While empiricism has its benefits, if taken to extremes it can also lead to disastrous consequences. If one needs 100% empirical proof to believe something, this will result in frustration and eventually **skepticism**[4].

Immediate sensory awareness is used to describe an immediate sensation as justification of a belief. This should not be confused with the concept of empiricism. Empiricism involves investigation, while immediate sense awareness is a sudden, unexamined sensation. For instance, if you claim, "I have a stomachache," then this is an immediate sensation. You did not have to investigate it; it is only a feeling, or sensation, that is obvious to you. Likewise, if you have felt that God is motivating you to do something, or even better, not to do something, this is an internal feeling that you have that does not necessarily have to be examined for you to justify this belief.

Criticism of Immediate Sensory Awareness- If you haven't noticed already, there is a serious problem with immediate sensory awareness. It's

[3] David Hume, *An Enquiry Concerning Human Understanding*, 5.1.

[4] Skepticism is the contention that we cannot truly know anything for sure. The skeptic must be skeptical about everything.

not verifiable. Take for example a story of a wife and her husband. Both of them begin a new exercise regimen with two separate personal trainers. After the first day of training they both come home sore and tired. The wife jokingly challenges the husband, "I am so much sorer than you are." Of course, there is no way of knowing who is sorer. To ache is a feeling that only you can feel. The husband and wife could not feel each other's pain in comparison to their own. The wife challenged the husband in such a way that neither of them could prove to be the victor. On a more basic level, you cannot prove to a friend that you have a stomachache. In the same way, it is difficult for someone to prove that God spoke to him, or that God exists because "I feel him in my heart." These sorts of claims are merely self evident, and in this sense of the term, these "sensations" are truly only evident to the self. Immediate sense awareness may be used to justify something for you, but is rarely helpful in an apologetic situation.

Summary

Knowledge has been defined as *justified true belief* or rather *a belief that corresponds to reality and has the justification to adequately prove it.* We all have ideas, some of which could be considered "knowledge." To determine what knowledge is and what it is not, we must recognize how we are to justify the belief in any given situation. We have seen the problems with looking to a poor source of information (authority), of using merely pure logic to find justification (rationality), with using solely our senses (empiricism) and claiming what is merely self evident to us (immediate sense awareness). It seems as though we must take every situation, discover the appropriate tests to see if the belief corresponds to reality and use our minds and our senses to justify or even to disqualify the belief from being considered "knowledge." *In most cases we should be using multiple categories to justify our beliefs.* It is often a pitfall if one tries to regulate his justifications to one sort.

The Relationship between Metaphysics, Truth, and Epistemology

Hopefully, by now you have noticed the relationship between metaphysics, truth, and epistemology. In metaphysics we consider what is real. Our view of truth is that which corresponds to reality, and our epistemology, or our knowledge, is dependent on what is true. These three areas of study are very similar to a four-story structure. With metaphysics (Realism) as our foundation, we are able to have a firm basis for truth, knowledge, and our justification of Christianity. For instance, why would an absolute idealist attempt to prove Christianity using physical evidence? If we believe that nothing is real and all is illusion, then our metaphysic will not even allow us to believe that Christ was truly real! Yet because we believe that there is an external reality, that we are able to know it, and understand some of it using our senses and mind, then and only then can we begin to give evidence for the existence of God and the accuracy of Christianity.

These first four chapters may have been a bit philosophical and abstract, yet without understanding the philosophical underpinnings of Christianity then we would be unable to justify our belief in theism, and more specifically, the person and work of Jesus Christ. See the foundation pyramid for more clarification:

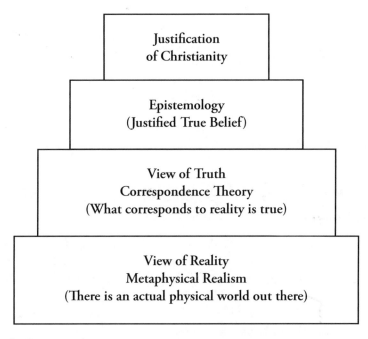

Justification
of Christianity

Epistemology
(Justified True Belief)

View of Truth
Correspondence Theory
(What corresponds to reality is true)

View of Reality
Metaphysical Realism
(There is an actual physical world out there)

Study Questions

WHICH ONE?

1. Define Knowledge using the sentence given in the chapter. Now describe knowledge using the three-word definition: explain each word in the definition.
2. Formulate examples for Authority, Rationality, Empiricism, and immediate sense awareness.

3. What is the difference between an *a priori* and *a posteriori* argument?
4. Explain why immediate sense awareness is not provable. Give an example.
5. Explain the "Foundation Pyramid" in your own words. Why does our view of metaphysics, epistemology, and truth affect our justification of Christianity?

Terms to Consider

Epistemology
Knowledge
Rationality
Syllogism
a priori
Analytical Statement
Empiricism
a posteriori
Skepticism
Immediate Sensory Awareness
Authority

Memory Verse Options

Proverbs 1:7

Going Beyond the Call of Duty: Readings for the Overachiever

College students:

Geisler, Norman and Paul Feinberg. *Introduction to Philosophy: A Christian Perspective.* Grand Rapids: Baker Book House, 1980.

Gilson, Etienne. *The Unity of Philosophical Experience.* New York: Charles Scribners Sons, 1937.

Owen, Joseph. *Cognition: An Epistemological Inquiry.* Notre Dame: University of Notre Dame Press, 1992.

High School students:

Palmer, Donald. *Looking at Philosophy.* Mountain View: Mayfield Publishing, 1988.

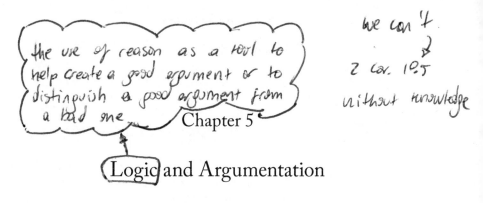

the use of reason as a tool to help create a good argument or to distinguish a good argument from a bad one

we can't
2 Cor. 10:5
without knowledge

Chapter 5

Logic and Argumentation

"A simple man believes anything,
but a prudent man gives thought to his steps."
—Proverbs 14:15

Why a Chapter on Logic and Argumentation?

WHILE IT may seem illogical to place a chapter on logic in the middle of an apologetics book, it must be understood that without a basic understanding of some logical principles you may be missing a foundational part of your apologetic. Since logic is the study of right reasoning, then without proper logic you may come to the wrong conclusions. Simply put, bad logic leads to bad conclusions. If your conclusions are wrong about reality, then what you claim to "know" may not be true-justified-belief at all!

Even though logic has been used extensively in the last four chapters, it has not been demonstrated how to make valid arguments and how to dismantle invalid ones. Since apologetics is the study devoted to the justification and defense of the Christian faith, then in order to be fully prepared to be an apologist you must understand these basics of logical reasoning.

While the study of logic can be intense and complex, the following paragraphs contain the less complex but also some of the most important facets of logical understanding. So do not be misled, the study of logic runs much deeper than the paragraphs that will follow. Logic can be applied to many different fields of study: science, mathematics, philosophy, religion, etc. It would be impossible for us to cover all the inferences and implications of this discipline in such a small section. This chapter will be regulated to five segments: what is logic, the two branches of logic, truth and validity, the anatomy of an argument, and other logical fallacies.

What Is Logic?

Dr. Norman Geisler explains in his *Come, Let us Reason*, "Logic is the study of right reason or valid inferences and the attending fallacies, formal and informal."[1] To put it in simpler terms, **logic is simply the use of reason** *p. 55* as a tool to help create a good argument or to distinguish a good argument from a bad one.

There should be no doubt that God has called us to reason out our beliefs, to be able to explain these reasons, and to lovingly point out flaws in the logic of others. Again, if 1 Peter 3:15 is taken into account, Christians are to "give the reason for the hope that you have. But do this with gentleness and respect." In 2 Corinthians 10:5 Paul writes that Christians are to "demolish arguments and every pretension that sets itself up against the knowledge of God." How are Christians to explain that our beliefs are without contradiction and to "demolish arguments" without having a basic knowledge of logic? It seems that the contents of this chapter, as well as further study of logic beyond this textbook, can only help the apologist fulfill his task and defend Christianity.

Two Branches of Logic

In the traditional study of logic, the subject is divided into two branches: **inductive** and **deductive** logic. There are two basic ways of telling these two branches apart. First of all, deductive logic results in a conclusive result, while inductive logic only supports, but does not prove the conclusion. Secondly, in most cases, deductive logic argues from the general to the specific, while inductive logic commonly argues from the specific to the general. For an example, look at these syllogisms:

Deductive Logic: a priori

All men are mortal (general)
Socrates is a man(specific)
Therefore, Socrates is mortal (specific)

This deductive argument is conclusive. In other words, no matter what else you say about Socrates, unless you deny premise one or two, then it is irrefutable that he is mortal. Also notice that the argument goes from general, "all men" to specific, "Socrates." On the other hand, the

Deductive: argues from general to specific, is conclusive

[1] Norman Geisler and Ron Brooks, *Come, let us reason: An introduction to logical thinking* (Baker Book House: Grand Rapids, 1990), 12.

inductive argument argues from specific to general and leaves the logician with an inconclusive result:

Inductive: from specific to general
— conclusion is not definitive

Inductive Logic: a posteri

Socrates is mortal (specific)
Fred is mortal (specific)
Jeff is mortal (specific)
Therefore, all men are mortal. (general)[2]

The inductive argument may give some evidence that all men are mortal, but the argument does not prove this conclusively. Now, this is an interesting argument because everyone knows that at some point everyone will die. So, it may seem weird to you that this argument isn't conclusive, so let's look at another:

Socrates likes badminton
Billy likes badminton
Fred likes badminton
Therefore, all men like badminton.

This argument can't be used to prove without a doubt that all men love badminton. In order to do that you would have to list *every* man in existence. Thus this sort of logic only gives evidence for a conclusion, but does not prove the result unequivocally. With this in mind, this chapter will focus on deductive logic. While some of Christian apologetics is inductive, the basis and foundational principles of logic are much easier to digest if discussed in a deductive framework. Therefore, in this chapter, the conclusion of each argument must either be conclusively true or conclusively false.

Truth and Validity

When anyone is presented with an argument, there are two characteristics that need to be considered in order to determine the argument's precision; they are truth and validity. Truth deals with whether the premises correspond to reality, while validity considers whether or not the logic involved in the argument is correct. This sounds pretty reasonable, but there is a bit

---

[2] It should be noted that it is possible, although rare, for a deductive argument to have only general premises, as well as an inductive argument to contain solely specific statements. Take for example the conclusion footnoted above. If "Therefore, all men are mortal" were to simply be replaced with "Therefore, Bill is mortal," this would be a specific conclusion, with specific premises. → *content*

2 TESTS: Is it true?
Is it valid? → ~~structure~~ logical structure

of a twist. You see, a bad argument can be logically valid, but not true; and another bad argument could be logically invalid and yet true. For instance, let's suggest this line of reasoning: the sun is 30 million miles away. Light travels at 186,212 miles per second. Thus it takes 2.5 minutes for sunlight to reach earth. What do you think?

Two questions must now be asked: is it valid? and is it true? The first of the two questions is correct. The logic involved in this argument is accurate. Yet one has to ask about each of the premises. Is the sun really 30 million miles away? No! It is actually more like 90 million miles away. Thus the conclusion is incorrect and the argument is rubbish.

I have given you an example of an argument with proper logic, yet with untrue premises. Let's look at an example with improper logic, yet a true conclusion: If Bunnies are furry animals, then Bears are furry animals too! Bears *are* furry animals. Therefore, Bunnies *must be* furry animals too! While this uses incorrect logic (see affirming the consequent in the hypothetical syllogism section below), the conclusion is actually true. Bunnies are very furry animals. While the conclusion does correspond to reality, this argument cannot be used to support this conclusion.

The Anatomy of an Argument

When the term "argument" is used in a logical sense the writer is not implying that there are two people in a heated verbal disagreement. A logician may write an argument with no one else around and with no one else to discuss it. An argument is simply a series of interconnected sentences that result in giving evidence for a conclusion. These sentences are not interconnected literally, but logically. One sentence logically leads to the next until you have proven your conclusion.

In logic, the structure of an argument is called a syllogism. A syllogism usually consists of at least three sentences, two being **premises** and the last being the **conclusion**. The argument below is a **categorical syllogism**. It is the easiest to distinguish and understand because the premises simply contain "This is that" or "This is not that" meanings. For example:

Premise 1 (called the major premise):
    The city of Charlotte is in North Carolina

Premise 2 (called the minor premise):
    North Carolina is in the United States

Conclusion:
    The City of Charlotte is in the United States

While this is a simple categorical argument placed into syllogistic form you can see that the premises do in fact prove the conclusion. If you are having problems understanding, the easiest way to grasp this method is to put the argument in a more formal arrangement. Take the last syllogism and break it into three parts, called terms. The first term, "Charlotte" will be the letter "A." The second term, "North Carolina" will be "B" and "USA" will be "C." If the syllogism is restructured with these letters instead of written out in sentences and it is placed in a circle diagram, the argument becomes even clearer:

A is B[3]
B is C
Therefore, A is C

Let's add a negative to this argument. Let us switch the term "USA" to "Russia" and deny that North Carolina is in Russia. Our argument would look like this:

North Carolina is not in Russia
The city of Charlotte is in North Carolina
The City of Charlotte is not in Russia

And the logical form of this argument would look like:

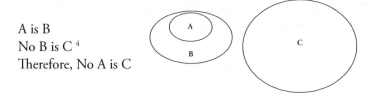

A is B
No B is C [4]
Therefore, No A is C

Notice that in categorical syllogisms, the conclusion MUST correspond to the circles you have drawn. If the circles and conclusion do correspond, the argument is valid; if not, it is invalid. For example,

---

[3] The "in" is implied here. It may help you to read these as "A is *in* B."

[4] Notice that the logical form does not read "B is not C" but rather No B is C. This is done simply for logical clarity. The wording in English may be considered awkward: "None of North Carolina is in Russia" and "None of the City of Charlotte is in Russia." While awkward in English, this way is the easiest way to comprehend the logical structure and to prevent error. (See the circle graph for an example.)

Valid:	*Invalid:* (see diagram)
A is B	A is C
B is C	B is C
Thus, A is C.	Thus, A is B.

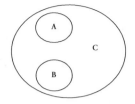

Valid:	*Invalid:*
Charlotte is in NC	Charlotte is in USA
NC is in the USA	NC is in USA
Charlotte is in USA	Thus, Charlotte is in NC[5]

Observe how the conclusion in the "Invalid" column above is actually true. Charlotte is truly in North Carolina. While this is the truth, you cannot prove this assertion with the argument above. The conclusion simply doesn't logically follow from the premises. The only logical conclusion that can be derived from both of these statements is "Both Charlotte and NC are in the USA."

Hypothetical arguments are some of the most used arguments in everyday life. Any time you use an "If/then" statement, you have stated a hypothetical. So when someone uses the phrase "hypothetically speaking" they simply mean, "if this was the case then . . . " Here is a classic example. I am sure you can remember back when you tried to bribe your parents into giving you something you wanted, "If I wash your car then will you let me go to Fred's house?"

Every hypothetical argument has two parts: an antecedent and a consequent. The antecedent is the section that comes right after the "if" and the consequent comes after the "then" statement. In the example in the previous paragraph, "wash your car" is the antecedent and "let me go to Fred's" is the consequent. Understanding the names of these two terms is crucial in order to comprehend the next section.

There are only two ways of logically proving that a hypothetical argument is valid: affirming the antecedent[6] or denying the consequent.[7] Let's take this for example:

"If there are absolute moral laws (antecedent)

then there must be a moral lawgiver (consequent)."

---

[5] This is formally known as the fallacy of "undistributed middle." The term C (or USA) does not refer to ALL of the members in its group (NC or Charlotte). Thus we cannot make a logical connection between NC and Charlotte.

[6] A.k.a. Modus Ponens.

[7] A.k.a. Modus Tollens.

Given this hypothetical statement, there are only <u>two ways for the</u> <u>learner to end up with a logically valid</u> conclusion. The <u>student could af-</u> <u>firm the antecedent "there are absolute moral laws" thus the consequent</u> <u>would be true as well:</u>

If there are absolute moral laws then there must be a moral lawgiver.
There are absolute moral laws
Thus, there must be a moral lawgiver.

<u>The only other</u> logical possibility is to deny the consequent, "There is *no* moral lawgiver." The conclusion then is there are no absolute moral laws:

If there are absolute moral laws then there must be a moral lawgiver.
There is not a moral lawgiver
Thus, there are no absolute moral laws.

This last argument may offend you, but remember, the logician is not dealing with proving truth here, but rather validity. At this point the logician just wants to make sure the logic is valid. It is up to the atheist to defend the claim that "There is no moral lawgiver." Only then would the above argument be logically valid AND true.

You may be thinking, "Well why can't I just deny the antecedent and affirm the consequent?" First and foremost, this would be very, very bad. Both of these are actually logical fallacies. Let's try a new example:

"If Jacob is eaten by a shark (antecedent)
then he will die young(consequent)."

Let's assume that a shark does not eat Jacob, and thus we have denied the antecedent:

Invalid:
If Jacob is eaten by a shark then he will die young.
Jacob is not eaten by a shark.
Therefore, Jacob will not die young.

It does not logically follow that Jacob will not die young. The problem in this situation is that there are other circumstances of which you haven't taken account. For instance, what if Jacob meets his unfortunate fate by being eaten by a rabid camel? While a silly illustration, it shows that just because Jacob is not eaten by a shark, this doesn't mean that he will have a long life!

TWO WAYS FOR HYPOTHETICAL SYLLOGISM TO BE LOGICAL:
a. affirming the antecedent
b. denying the consequent

Likewise, if you affirm the consequent, the same sorts of problems arise. Let's affirm, "Jacob will die young":

Invalid:

If Jacob is eaten by a shark then he will die young.
Jacob will die young
Therefore, Jacob will be eaten by a shark.

Does it logically follow that Jacob MUST have been eaten by a shark? Not at all! Maybe that rabid camel is on the loose again! It may be morbid to mention the number of unfortunate ways that Jacob could meet his fate, but the point has been made, no matter the circumstance, you cannot deny the antecedent or affirm the consequent and have a logical and undeniable conclusion.

The last types of syllogisms discussed in this chapter are **disjunctive syllogisms**. Disjunctive syllogisms are simply "Either/Or" statements. For example: "Either I am going to eat eggs OR I am going to eat pancakes." Before analyzing this example, you have to agree that at least one of the options is true and in most cases both options could be true![8] For instance, I could affirm, "I am eating pancakes," and you cannot deduce whether I am eating eggs or not! Couldn't I decide to fix both and eat them together? The only way to logically conclude with certainty is to deny one of the two options.

Either I am going to eat eggs OR I am going to eat pancakes.
I am not going to eat eggs.
Therefore, I am going to eat pancakes.

Since I have denied the first alternate, "I am not going to eat eggs," then one can logically deduce that I am having pancakes. Of course, this would work the other way around as well. I could deny that I am going to eat pancakes, and then you could deduce that I am going to eat eggs. This logical procedure is widely used when one uses the "process of elimination" in multiple-choice tests. All the student has to do is eliminate the other possibilities (deny each alternate) until only one is left. The one that is left MUST be the right answer. The disjunctive syllogism is one where one can only deny an alternate in order to find a valid conclusion. Affirming an alternate, then denying the other, is not an option.

---

[8] This is true unless we are in a situation such as an excluded middle: "Either I am eating eggs, or I am not eating eggs." If this is the case, then both of the options cannot be true!

Other Logical Fallacies

While many fallacies would be considered "formal fallacies," such as denying the antecedent in a hypothetical syllogism or affirming an alternate in a disjunctive syllogism, what are provided in the rest of the chapter are a few "informal fallacies" to whet your mental taste buds. What you will find below are several common fallacies that occur in everyday illogical arguments.

Straw man—Of course, a straw man in reality is not an actual man, but rather is a false representation of a man. Thus a straw man fallacy occurs when one misrepresents another person's view, and then slams that misrepresentation. For instance, in Bertrand Russell's *Why I am not a Christian* he states that "If everything must have a cause, then God must have a cause."[9] Russell is saying that since Christians believe that everything has a cause, then God must have a cause as well. Russell happily set up a straw man that falsely reflected our position and proceeded to knock it down. This is a straw man fallacy due to the fact that Christians do not believe that "everything must have a cause," rather Christians believe that everything that has a beginning has a cause. God does not have a beginning, so he does not need a cause.

Begging the Question (aka Petitio Principii or a Circular Argument)—This fallacy occurs when the argument contains the conclusion within the premises of the argument. Unfortunately, this is a fallacy of which Christians often become accused, and more unfortunately, the accusations are usually justified. Here are a few examples:

> Freida says: How do you know that the Bible is true?
> Billy says: The Bible is God's Word and you have to trust God's Word.
> Freida: ok . . . so . . .
> Billy replies: Well if God's Word says that the Bible is true, then it must be true!

This example reworded looks like this:

The Bible is the Word of God.
The Word of God is true.
Thus, the Bible is true.

---

[9] Bertrand Russell, *Why I am not a Christian*, 6.

The major problem with this argument is that every Christian knows that when one says the term "Word of God" then it is the Bible; it is simply a synonym. So, what the actual argument reads is:

The Bible is the Bible.
The Bible is true.
Thus, the Bible is true.

Looking at it this way you can see that premise 2 and the conclusion are the same. This is begging the question. You cannot imply the conclusion, either explicitly or implicitly, in one of the premises. Begging the Question does nothing to convince the skeptic; in fact, it usually infuriates him. If he asks, "Does God exist?" you should not reply, "Yes, God says so in the Bible." In referring to the Bible you are already assuming that God exists and are not giving any objective evidence. In addition, you have probably offended the skeptic to the point that he will not respect anything else you have to say.[10]

Poisoning the Well—This fallacy occurs when one who is speaking states a claim that would make anything else his opponent says sound utterly foolish. For instance, if speaking with an atheist in front of a group of people I may say, "Psalm 51:3 reads, 'the fool says in his heart, 'There is no God.'" Now this may be a true statement, but it would make everything else the atheist said seem foolish. For whenever the atheist tried to make his point, the audience would simply think back to this claim, "Only fools are atheists." While it may be fun for some to watch an atheist get fuming mad, it is not Christ-like, nor does it foster logical discussion.

As another example, in Canada there was a House of Commons Debate concerning abortion where one of the women of the house claimed that she wished there were more women who were members of that governmental committee so that they could speak on the issue. Her implication was that the men of the house could not fully understand the issue of abortion. She had poisoned the well. The men of the house could no longer speak up without this cloud of "Am I qualified to speak on this matter?" hanging over their heads.

Red Herring—This term got its name from when hunters would train their dogs to find prey. The hunter would first drag a rabbit across the ground (without the dogs present) and would then let the dog follow the scent of the animal. On the second try, the hunter would do the same ac-

---

[10] This sort of argument is only valid if you have already given evidence that the Bible is reliable.

tion, yet this time around he would drag a smoked herring across the trail where the rabbit had been dragged. The hunter then would let the dog go, hoping that the red herring scent would not throw off the dog's hunt for the rabbit.

In logic, the red herring fallacy occurs when one is asked a question and instead of taking the question directly, the person brings up a totally different subject. This fallacy often occurs in presidential debates. If the nominees are asked a question that they don't want to answer, they often will simply bring up an alternative subject and attempt to diffuse the query so they may simply move on to the next series of questions.

Post hoc—A *post hoc* argument arises when one argues that just due to the fact that a thing appears before a given event, that this thing caused this event to happen. For example, someone may claim, "I had a cold and so I took vitamin A. Now my cold is gone!" This person is suggesting that since he took vitamin A, this caused his cold to go away. But just because he took vitamin A before the cold went away, doesn't mean that the vitamin had anything to do with his cure. He has to show a causal relationship between the vitamin and the cure for his proof to be logical. If it were true that you could imply a causal relationship by simply stating what happened before an event, then one could believe that a rooster crowing causes the sun to rise and the singing of the national anthem causes a sporting event to begin.

False Dilemma (aka Third Option or Tertium Quid)—The fallacy of false dilemma occurs when one person offers his opponent a question and gives only a couple possible answers when there is actually a third option that is not mentioned. If the options given for the answer are exhaustive, then there is no fallacy. For instance, Shakespeare's famous dictum "to be or not to be" is not a fallacy. You only have two options: existence or non-existence. You cannot partially exist. Yet when a person suggests that there are only two possible solutions to a problem when actually there are more options that he is not mentioning, the fallacy of false dilemma has occurred. Take an example from scripture. After Jesus heals a blind man, Jesus' disciples ask him in John 9:2–3, "Rabbi, who sinned, this man or his parents, that he was born blind?" Jesus informs them that there was a third option that they had not considered, "Neither this man nor his parents sinned," said Jesus, "but this happened so that the work of God might be displayed in his life."

Hasty Generalization—When a person makes a conclusion based on too small a sampling of a group, then a hasty generalization has been made. You have already seen an example of a hasty generalization within this chapter:

Socrates likes badminton.
Billy likes badminton.
Fred likes badminton.
Therefore, all men like badminton.

It does not seem like the creator of this argument has done enough random sampling of men to establish that every man in existence could enjoy the sport of badminton. Of course, the question of "what is the key percentage to determine a proper generalization" may be asked. Since there is no definite answer, you should only declare "hasty generalization" when it is obvious.

Ad hominem—This fallacy literally means an argument "against the man." When this fallacy has been committed, the guilty party has taken the low road in the debate. Instead of discussing the issue, he has tried to assassinate the character of his opponent. At any time when a person involved in the debate is criticized instead of an issue in the argument, this fallacy has been committed. For instance, suppose a person is speaking to a city council about proposed changes in city planning, and someone in the crowd screams, "Sit down, you drunkard!" Now whether he is the town drunkard or not, it doesn't matter. What does matter is if his argument is logical and relevant to the issue at hand. (Of course, if he is drunk at the time then his argument is probably not sensical.)

Slippery Slope—One is accused of committing a slippery slope fallacy when it is claimed, "If you do this, then you will soon slip into that." This fallacy only occurs when an if/then statement is not causally related. For instance, if one states, "If we allow the government to restrict who can buy a gun, then pretty soon no one will be able to own a gun." This is simply not true. It is possible that the government could have some rational restrictions on gun ownership, yet not restrict to the point that no one can buy a gun.

Faulty Analogy—As the name denotes, this fallacy transpires when one makes an analogy that just doesn't unite the two things being compared. For example, "Believing in God is like believing in Santa Claus." Now this is ridiculous. Santa is not a supposed cause of the existence of the universe. Mr. Claus is not likely the standard for which our entire moral compass is founded. Christians have credible evidence that it is highly possible that God exists, yet bits and pieces of Santa's cookies and milk were

- Character Assassination
- Appeal to Popularity
- Genetic Fallacy

suspiciously on the chin of our father on Christmas morning. The analogy simply doesn't fly.

Summary

Most of us can tell when an argument "smells fishy" yet you may not know exactly what is wrong. Some may be content to state "that's illogical" then move on to the next argument. Yet if you are discussing these arguments with real people in a real conversation, you need to be able to explain *how and why* the argument is incorrect so as to lovingly help them discover the truth. This is why any student of apologetics and the Bible should be encouraged to study logic as well. Without this invaluable tool, rational thinking does not exist, and explaining the irrationality of a bad argument is impossible.

Study Questions

1. In your own words, define logic.
2. Contrast the two branches of logic.
3. Find an example of one of the "other logical fallacies" in a newspaper or on the Internet. Bring this article in with you for our next class. Remember to write down what fallacy has been committed and underline where the fallacy is in the article.
4. Explain the difference between truth and validity.
5. If you are given a hypothetical syllogism, *explain* the two ways that you can prove an argument to be valid.
6. *Describe* the two fallacies that can occur with hypothetical syllogisms.
7. If you are given a disjunctive syllogism, *explain* how you can prove this type of argument to be valid.

[handwritten margin note: EMAIL, BUT DON'T HAVE TO]

Terms to Consider

Logic
Deductive Logic
Inductive Logic
Argument
Syllogism
Premise
Conclusion
Categorical Syllogism
Hypothetical Syllogism

Valid:
> Affirming the Antecedent
> Denying the Consequent

Invalid:
> Affirming the Consequent
> Denying the Antecedent

Disjunctive Syllogism
Valid:
> Denying an alternate

Invalid:
> Affirming an alternate

Memorize the ten informal fallacies

Memory Verse Options

> Proverbs 14:15
> 2 Corinthians 10:5

Going Beyond the Call of Duty: Readings for the Overachiever

College Students:

Copi, Irving M. *Introduction to Logic.* New York: Macmillan Publishing, 1982.

High School Students:

Geisler, Norman, and Brooks, R. M. *Come, Let Us Reason: An Introduction to Logical Thinking.* Grand Rapids: Baker Books, 1990.

A.K.A.

Chapter 6

Investigating Worldviews

"From now on we regard no one from a worldly point of view.
Though we once regarded Christ in this way, we do so no longer."[1]
—The Apostle Paul

What Is a Worldview?

WHETHER THEY acknowledge it or not, all humans have a world-view. Everyone has his own perspective on central issues concerning reality. Three of these questions have already been considered: Is reality real? What is truth? How do you know what you know? Each of these will be answered differently by various people and will change the way that they look at the world. For instance, if a person believes that the world is *maya*, or an illusion, then he will look at the world much differently than a Christian who would state that everything is real and has been created by Almighty God.

There are many more questions that will be considered in detail over the remainder of this book that have huge implications on a person's worldview, such as the existence of God and the divinity of Christ. After these central questions are answered, these beliefs serve as a strainer for all information that comes in contact with each person. Your worldview is simply a web of beliefs that allows certain information to flow through as "truth" and other statements to be rejected as false. Imagine a conversation between a believer in God and an atheist. The believer tells his atheist friend about a miracle he witnessed; his grandmother had been miraculously healed. The atheist, who doesn't believe in miracles, immediately and without investigation rejects this statement as untrue. Miracles do not fit into his worldview! The statement became trapped in his "strainer" and did not pass through as truth.

A SET OF PRESUPPOSITIONS A PERSON USES TO INTERPRET THE UNIVERSE.

---

[1] 2 Cor. 5:16.

Which Worldview Is the Truth?

Some people believe that one cannot know which worldview is the truth. Because you were nurtured in a specific environment, you likely accept the worldview of those around us. Statistically, there is a lot of truth in the second part of the last statement. You are likely Christian, Mormon, Buddhist, what have you, because of your upbringing. Dr. Christian Smith, in his book *Soul Searching*, concludes that, "About three in four teens in the United States consider their own religious beliefs somewhat or very similar to their parents."[2]

The problem with this is that when we examine other worldviews, our personal worldview limits us from being objective in determining which worldview really does correspond to reality. All you have to do to realize this issue is to visit someone who has a totally different belief system than your own. If they are from a different culture, they may eat, dress, and act very differently than the Christian Americans around whom you grew up. Immediately, you may regard their beliefs about God, the after-life, and moral issues, as wrong, just based on the fact that they are different from you.

The question, then, is simple; can you be objective about worldviews? Can you set your worldview aside and deliberate the truth claims of each system, even your own? Is it possible for anyone to change his or her worldview?

It should be admitted that the young and immature adolescent may not be able to be objective about his religious belief, but there is no doubt that the older you get, the more you are able think intellectually about each worldview. The people that claim that a person can never be objective about worldviews do not have the facts on their side. There are people who change their worldviews everyday! There are Buddhists becoming Christians, Hindus who become Muslims, and even Christians turning to New Age ideas. The fact is, changes in worldviews do happen. A very well known philosopher has changed his worldview in the last decade. Antony Flew, one of the most famous atheists in the world, became a deist in 2004.[3] He had written 80 books and articles from the atheistic worldview, but now he believes that God exists! This was not an easy decision for Flew. He went from being a respected individual in the atheistic community, to being mocked and ridiculed by his former colleagues. People, even the staunchest of atheists, can change their worldview!

[2] Christian Smith, *Soul Searching* (New York: Oxford, 2005), 34.

[3] see Antony Flew and Gary Habermas, "My Pilgrimage from Atheism to Theism," *Philosophia Christi*, Vol. 6, No. 2 (2004) 197–212.

The underlying problem with the topic of worldviews is that most people have simply assumed their worldview and have never taken the time to personally to find reasons why they believe and why they have rejected the other perspectives. Given this problem, the rest of this chapter will deal with the seven most prevalent worldviews. While looking over these worldviews, attempt to be objective, rational, and express these thoughts in constructive ways. Just because something is "different" or "weird" doesn't make it wrong. What does make a view incorrect is when it contains logical contradictions and problems at its core.

The Seven Most Prevalent Worldviews

Each of these seven worldviews attempts to answer life's most meaningful questions. These questions are the focus of many philosopher's compositions and speeches, yet you will find that these are not mere scholar's issues, but issues that concern every man and woman in existence. This list of questions is not exhaustive and it is likely you will see longer and shorter versions of this list, yet this specific list includes the most critical of the issues:

1. Is there a God or any supernatural being? (Theology)
2. What is real? Is reality real? (Metaphysics)
3. What are the origins of man and the universe? (Cosmogony)
4. What is my meaning and purpose in life? (Teleology)
5. How do I know what is right and wrong? (Ethics, Axiology and Morality)
6. What is my destiny after death? (Eschatology and Immortality)
7. What is truth? How can I know it? (Epistemology)
8. What is the state of man? Is he good or sinful? (Anthropology)

Proponents of each of the worldviews below will have their take on all of these issues. How they answer these questions will effect your decision concerning which worldview holds the most credible view of the reality. Notice that none of the worldviews are "religions" per se, but each of the world's religions can be classified under one of the following worldviews.

Naturalism

These first two worldviews operate under the category of "naturalism" or "materialism." Both atheism and agnosticism deny that ANYTHING spiritual exists. Of course, neither affirms that a supernatural being exists, nor do they affirm that man has any spiritual element. So, they deem that man does not have a soul. Notice the implications that this presents when one considers the question, "What is my destiny after death?" If there is no soul, then there is no afterlife. When you die, you die. Ironically, atheists and agnostics are generally arrogant on this issue. They see the finality of death as something to be heroically accepted, as a brave warrior accepts his own fate in battle. Isaac Asimov, a twentieth century atheist and science fiction writer claims, "I can't help but believe that eternal happiness would eventually be boring. I cannot grasp the notion of eternal anything. My own way of thinking is that after death there is nothingness. Nothingness is the only thing that I think is worth accepting."[4]

Atheism : main focus is freedom.

Naturalism

Examination—An atheist is one who simply believes that God does not exist. Isaac Asimov writes, "I am an atheist, out and out. It took me a long time to say it. I've been an atheist for years and years, but somehow I felt it was intellectually unrespectable to say one was an atheist, because it assumed knowledge that one didn't have. Somehow, it was better to say one was a humanist or an agnostic. I finally decided that I'm a creature of emotion as well as of reason. Emotionally, I am an atheist. I don't have the evidence to prove that God doesn't exist, but I so strongly suspect he doesn't that I don't want to waste my time."[5] The atheist argues that he has enough reasons to believe that God does not exist. Thus Christians should not believe in God any more than they should believe that Santa Claus exists. How does an atheist go about proving that God does not exist?

"no absolute morals, cannot argue w/ Hitler

This is a tough question that atheists have been debating for decades. Generally speaking, proving a universal negative is almost always improbable. Take for instance the aforementioned claim that Santa Claus does not exist. How could you prove this? Even if you searched everywhere, Santa could have moved from place to place to avoid your detection. In a sense, you would have to be an omnipresent being in order to prove a universal negative.[6] This problem becomes even more problematic when dealing with God due to the fact that God is Spirit[7] Of course, atheists

---

[4] Paul Kurtz, "A Call for the Critical Examination of the Bible and Religion; Interview with Isaac Asimov on Science and the Bible," *Free Inquiry* 2, no. 2 (Spring 1982): 9.

[5] Ibid., 9.

[6] This does not apply to perfect induction. I could say "I do not have any coins in my pocket" and this could be quickly verified without problem.

[7] John 4:24.

have reasoned that this approach is useless and have taken on a different course of action.

Atheists focus their attention on showing that our concept of God contains contradictions. The atheist contends that if the concept of God has problems, then God can't exist after all. For instance, one of the greatest complaints against theism is that if God is all-powerful and all good, then why does evil exist? This topic is so significant that there is an entire chapter of this book devoted to it. Along the same lines, some atheists devote most of their attention to proving that the proofs argued for God's existence are somewhat faulty or totally unfounded. Even if these claims are true, they still do not prove the non-existence of God; but they would knock the feet out from under the evidence for theism.

Critique—The critiques of atheism are three-fold. First, atheists do not give adequate reasons for believing that God does not exist. Even Isaac Asimov in the quote above admits that he doesn't have the evidence to prove it; he simply suspects that God doesn't exist. Does this seem intellectually unbiased to you? It seems that the atheists have blind faith in their beliefs just as much, or more than, the theist. They simply do not have adequate arguments for the non-existence of God.

Secondly, atheists do not prove that our concept of God includes fatal contradictions. While the arguments for God's existence, the critiques of these arguments, and the problem of evil have not yet been discussed, let it be known that the atheist arguments against our concept of God fall flat.

Thirdly, atheists do not have reasonable answers when asked questions concerning ethics and purpose in life. Ethically speaking, atheists have no objective moral standard to build a moral edifice. Why is cheating wrong? Why shouldn't I go partying and get drunk? Christians have God as a basis for what is right and wrong, or good and bad. God is good. He is our standard. In revealing himself to us, he shows us who he is and what is correct behavior. When atheists attempt to explain their foundation for morals it usually tends to result in relativism. Atheists also struggle with explaining our purpose in life. The major problem is that purpose signifies design and design denotes that there is a designer. If you have ever wondered "Why am I here?" you are implying that some intellectual being put you here for a reason; you have a purpose in life. An atheist could only consider that he creates his own purpose, yet is this a purpose at all? Can he have designed himself for a goal, before he even existed? No. It seems that on these two issues alone atheism is an implausible worldview.

[handwritten margin note: impossible to prove, morally undesirable]

Agnosticism

Examination—Agnosticism derives its name from two Greek words ("*a*" which means "no," and "*gnosis*" which means knowledge.) An agnostic is one who does not know anything about the existence of God. Now there are two breeds of this worldview: benign and malignant agnostics. The benign agnostic simply says, "I don't know anything about the existence of God." A person who falls into this category may even be open for discussion concerning the proofs for God's existence and may come to Christ soon enough. The malignant agnostic is much more complex. He states, "No one can know if God exists." He is stating that he does not know, but also, *you* cannot know anything about God. They submit that it is impossible to have knowledge about the existence of God.

In his statement above, Asimov stated that for non-believers, "it was better to say one was . . . an agnostic." Why is this the case? There are two reasons. First, most naturalists have realized the problem with atheism; namely, they cannot prove that God does not exist. Secondly, converting to agnosticism puts the burden of proof back on the theist. The theist, instead of simply stating, "prove to me God doesn't exist," now must answer the question, "How can one know that God exists?" The agnostic has turned the tables and now the theist must do the talking.

Bertrand Russell, one of the most notorious agnostics of our time wrote, "I do not pretend to be able to prove that there is no God. I equally cannot prove that Satan is a fiction. The Christian God may exist; so may the gods of Olympus, or of ancient Egypt, or of Babylon. But no one of these hypotheses is more probable than any other: they lie outside the region of even probable knowledge, and therefore there is no reason to consider any of them."[8] The agnostic simply argues that since you cannot be sure about the existence of God, then no one should discuss him or assume that he exists. Arguing for God's existence is a waste of time, and the agnostic views theism as utterly unreasonable.

Critique—Before moving on to any new critiques, remember that agnosticism, like atheism, does not adequately answer the question of ethical foundations and one's purpose in life. In atheism there is no conception of supernatural on which to base our morals, nor is there an intelligent being who designs us for a specific purpose. Bertrand Russell himself stated, "I do not think that life in general has any purpose. It just happened."[9]

---

[8] Bertrand Russell, *Why I am not a Christian*, 50–51.
[9] Ibid., 79.

While this is a heavy blow against the school of agnosticism, there is one more critique to follow. But before looking at this critique you must understand this philosophical principle: In order to know what something is not, you must know something about what it truly is. For instance, until recently my wife would often lose her keys in our house. Ironically, she would often notice that she had misplaced them right before she needed to leave for a big meeting or something else of importance. I would often rush around the house looking for these keys. It would always baffle me when I would go into a specific part of the house and she would tell me, "No! They are not in there." Being the over-analytical philosopher that I am, I would think to myself, "How does she know where the keys are not, if she doesn't know where they are?" How does this apply to agnosticism? Agnostics claim that you cannot know anything about God, especially his existence. Yet agnostics do claim that they know something about God. Agnostics claim that God is unknowable. Isn't this a claim about the nature of God? They would have to know this truth about God in order to know that he is unknowable.

Here is another example. If someone made the claim "Humans cannot hear high pitch frequencies," how could they justify this claim? They would have to obtain a dog whistle, put a series of persons in a soundproof room and have each subject blow the whistle. If the whistle blower could not hear the sound, then this claim would be justified. Now, in order to "know" if humans cannot perceive the sound, the sound MUST exist in order to make the claim valid. In the case of agnostics, in order to be empirically justified in their belief, they have to believe in the existence of God in order to *know* that we cannot know him. But how can they claim that no human could know or sense God unless we have some sort of experiment like the one above?

Supernaturalism

The worldviews classified under the title of supernaturalism agree on one thing: there is a thing or being that they call "God." Now each will have a different conception of God, yet when questioned, all would agree that there is a God or gods.

Before going further there needs to be a short discussion on two words that will pepper the critiques of these worldviews. These words are **finite** and **infinite**. These words can simply be translated as 'limited in perfection' and 'unlimited in perfection.' The contention of the theist is that the God of all creation must be an infinite being who is unlimited perfection. This being contains all of the perfections possible; in fact, traditional theists would say that he *is* perfection. In other words, he is the standard by which humans know what is good, evil, wise, powerful, just, and loving. If this being is not unlimited in perfection, he is thus imperfect and cannot be God.

It must be realized that all of these perfections, in some way, are all bound together in God. If God is limited in some way, or in *any* way, then he is no longer infinite. For instance, let us suggest that God is not eternal. Eternality is simply the concept that God is outside of time. He does not go through history as his creation does; he sees history as a timeline. He does not live in a moment-by-moment existence. He may know what "present tense" is for us, but he is not limited by time. Let's now turn the tables and suggest that God does live in our moment-by-moment existence and is limited by time. If this were the case, he could not know the future. The future has not yet occurred, and he is trapped in the present. Thus, if God is not eternal then he cannot be omniscient. The tidal wave of imperfection continues on from there. For instance, if God is not omniscient, then neither is he omnipotent. For if he does not know what effects his power will have on the future, how can his power be truly effective? He may intend on doing something good with his power, but he didn't realize, because he doesn't know the future, that his action was going to have disastrous consequences. Now, if his power could produce disastrous consequences, could this being be all-good? I think you are getting the idea. If a being is not infinite, or unlimited perfection, then he is not perfect in any sense of the word. Lastly, it will become plainly evident in our section on the Cosmological Argument that if God is not infinite, then he needs a creator. If he is limited in any way, he must also be limited in his existence; and he would depend on another for his creation and sustenance.

Pantheism

Examination—Pantheists are an interesting lot due to the fact that they do posit that God exists, but he is not an intellectual being. Rather, everything is god. The trees are god, the fish are god, birds are god, and even you are god! Pantheism derives its name from two words "pan" meaning all or everything, and "theism," meaning god. All is god. God and the universe are one being. Depending on the pantheist to whom you talk, they will have different conceptions about their relation to the universe and their unity to God. Pantheism is unlike other theistic worldviews because there is no personality for us to pray to or ask advice. Most pantheists would claim that there is a "force" of God, but this is not a person, but is merely what some call Mother Nature.

The role of humanity is to simply understand their part in the universe and commune with nature. Robert Fulghum, author of the widely acclaimed book *All I Really Need to Know I Learned in Kindergarten*, writes in his article "Pay Attention," "If someone were to ask me whether I believed in God, or saw God, or had a particular relationship with God, I would reply that I don't separate God from my world in my thinking. I feel that God is everywhere. That's why I never feel separated from God or feel I must seek God, any more than a fish in the ocean feels it must seek water. In a sense, God is the 'ocean' in which we live."[10]

Abner Kneeland, a nineteenth century Unitarian Universalist believed "that the whole universe is NATURE, and that the word NATURE embraces the whole universe, and that God and Nature, so far as we can attach any rational idea to either, are perfectly synonymous terms. Hence I am not an Atheist, but a Pantheist; that is, instead of believing there is no God, I believe that in the abstract, all is God; and that all power that is, is in God, and that there is no power except that which proceeds from God."[11]

To the pantheist, God is infinite. Nature is perfect and is unlimited perfection. The changes and evil that occur in our everyday living are merely illusions that should not be taken seriously. The most notable advocates of Pantheism are Hindus, some Buddhists, and those in the New Age movement.

Critique—Pantheists argue that God is infinite and claim that it, by nature, is unchanging and perfect. Pantheists realize that if God changes, then it can no longer be perfect. For if something that is completely perfect changes, the only way it can change is from perfection to imperfection. So the pantheist must argue that change is simply an illusion. The only problem is that pantheists do not have a response to the question, "How do you know that you are not a part of the illusion?" Everyone changes. You grow, learn, and move. These are changes that happen every day. So how can humanity be infinite? In fact, if humans were truly infinite, they would all be omniscient. To be completely and perfectly infinite, each of us would have to have unlimited knowledge. Yet each of us learns and changes his mind. Another example of change is death. There is no doubt, no matter your

---

[10] Richard Carlson and Benjamin Shield, eds., *Handbook of the Soul* (Boston: Little, Brown and Company, 1995), 10.

[11] Abner Kneeland, In a letter written at Hebron, New Hampshire, May 28, 1833.

worldview, that death is a major change in one's being. So is death merely an illusion as well? It seems that these questions remain unanswered.

Lastly, if the world was infinite, it could not have ever begun to exist, and the universe would have to have existed forever. Science contradicts this assertion and states that the world had a beginning. Yet, if it had a beginning, it must have had a creator, due to the fact that it could not have started itself. The world cannot be infinite in any sense of the word.

Deism

Examination—A deist argues that a God exists; yet the deity does not interfere with his creation. In a sense, he is like a clockmaker who "wound up" his clock and is now letting it run on its own. Many theological contradictions would occur if you attempted to be a Christian deist. For instance, the god of deism has made the laws of this universe and will not break these laws; thus the deist does not believe in miracles or answered prayer. Likewise, since God could not have gotten involved here on earth, this renders Jesus' divinity a sham.

There are actually a couple famous deists in American history: Ben Franklin and Thomas Jefferson. You may notice that these deists, as well as the deists that lived before them, were well acquainted with the current scientific scene. They viewed the laws of nature as steadfast, unbreakable principles that could not even be broken by their creator. They felt that scientifically, God was limited from involving himself with his own creation. While deism experienced growth during the scientific explosion in the seventeenth to nineteenth centuries, it has since declined.

Critique—While intelligent men in recent history believed in deism, it seems as though the worldview is actually very unreasonable. For instance, why couldn't a being that created the world out of nothing part a sea? Why couldn't the being who designed all of creation participate in that creation? Could it be asserted that creation itself was a miracle that involved God in his creation?

All of these speculations aside, there are two clear-cut critiques that can be asserted. First, if the god of deism is not able to act in his own creation then this being is not an unlimited, infinite being. He does not even have the power to act in a realm in which he is architect. Therefore, the god of deism is not omnipotent, he is not all-powerful, and thus he is not infinite.

Secondly, one of the major reasons that deists were deists during the surge in science was due to their perception of scientific laws. Scientists once thought that the laws of nature were steadfast and unbreakable.

Modern scientists do not view the scientific laws as hardened fact. Today, scientists treat the scientific laws more as general laws, not universal ones. Anomalies, while rare, are simply times when a deviation from a scientific law occurs in nature. Since this has been realized, those who would classify themselves as deists have steadily dwindled.

Polytheism

Examination—Polytheism is the view that there are many finite gods that exist in the world. Unlike monotheism and deism, these gods are not beyond the world but only function within the realm of the universe. One of the major issues with polytheists is the origination of the world. Instead of God creating the world out of nothing, polytheists claim that these finite beings organized and designed the world out of already existing material. Take for instance Joseph Smith, the founder of Mormonism, and his account of the origin of the world:

> In the beginning, the head of the Gods called a council of the Gods: and they came together and concocted a plan to create the world and people it. . . . Now, I ask all who hear me, why the learned men who are preaching salvation, say that God created the heavens and the earth out of nothing? The reason is, that they are unlearned in the things of God, and have not the gift of the Holy Ghost . . . If you tell them that God made the world out of something, they will call you a fool. But I am learned, and know more than all the world put together . . . Hence we infer that God had materials to organize the world out of chaos—chaotic matter, which is element . . . Element had an existence from the time he [God] had. The pure principles of element are principles which can never be destroyed: they may be organized and reorganized, but not destroyed. They had no beginning, and can have no end.[12]

A creation *ex nihilo,* or creation out of nothing, does not exist in the thought of polytheists. They are content to believe in a timeless and endless nature of the universe.

Usually, these gods have some power over specific parts of the universe. Take Greek mythology for example, where Poseidon was the god of the sea and Aphrodite was the god of love. Each god has a sphere of dominion.[13] While there may be a hierarchy in these traditions, there is never a God who is an infinite being.

[12] Joseph Smith, *Teachings of the Prophet Joseph Smith* (Salt Lake City: Deseret Book Co., 1977), 349–52.

[13] Roman and Greek mythology is actually a specific form of polytheism called Henotheism.

Critique—The biggest problem with polytheism deals with the question "What is the origin of all things?" In monotheism there is an infinite God who is the creator of everything else. He has no beginning and needs no beginning. Yet in the polytheistic worldview, all of their gods are admittedly finite. They actually have a beginning; something created them. Usually a polytheist would remark that these gods came from the matter that already existed. Yet this creates two major problems: First, if nature existed before these gods, and nature created these gods, why not worship nature? In this case wouldn't nature be more worthy of worship than these godlike figures? Secondly, polytheists have never given a decent account of how the matter that was used to organize this universe came into existence. How did the raw materials used to create the universe come into existence in the first place? The origin of matter is never explained.

Last, the polytheist has trouble giving an account of the objectivity of his ethics. For instance, if there are a multitude of gods who are giving him commands, how is he to know which one to follow? What if multiple gods give conflicting commands? Let's suggest that one person's god gives the mandate, "Lying is wrong," then another person is given a command by his god, "Lying is not wrong." Would it then be possible to have absolute truth? No. Neither of the polytheists in the example above would have a strict moral and ethical standard by which to judge what is right and wrong. They simply would judge based on their own feelings and opinions. Thus, in some cases, polytheism ends in relativism.

Finite Godism

Examination—Adherents to finite godism contend that one or more areas of God's nature are finite. To a particular finite godist, God may be omnibenevolent but not omnipotent. To another, God may be omnipotent but not omniscient. Some would even say that God is a good being, but is limited because he somehow depends on the world.[14] Those who fit in this worldview may have somewhat differing views of God, yet they all unite under the conclusion that there is a God but that he is not a perfectly unlimited being. Rather, something in his nature is lacking perfection.

One of the most common complaints of the finite godist is the problem of evil. John Stuart Mill writes, "These particulars are important, because they show that my father's rejection of all that is called religious belief, was not, as many might suppose, primarily a matter of logic and

This occurs when there are a multitude of gods, with one superior yet finite god.

[14] This branch of finite godism is called "Panentheism" and was proposed by Alfred North Whitehead.

evidence: the grounds of it were moral, still more than intellectual. He found it impossible to believe that a world so full of evil was the work of an Author combining infinite power with perfect goodness and righteousness."[15] Since Mill did not think that the rebuttals to the problem of evil were sufficient, he deemed that if God exists at all, he must be lacking in his omnibenevolence or omnipotence.

In the last few years another type of finite godism has come to fruition. A few Christian scholars have deemed that God's omniscience infringes on the freedom of his creation. Therefore, if God were truly omniscient, our actions would be fatally determined. Each person would have no choice in any matter; you would have to do what God knew you were going to do. This unorthodox belief has led to "Open Theism," the view that God does not know the future acts of free creatures. This view has limited the knowledge of God, and has also has limited him to the realm of time.[16]

Critique—The major critique of finite godism is quite obvious: God cannot be finite. If God is finite in any way shape or form, this leads to a God who has the capability to change and who needs a creator. Even if God is limited in the minutest of ways, he would be a being who changes and is not the creator of the universe.

Secondly, if God changes or simply has the capability to change, the finite godist cannot base his ethics on this being. If a standard changes, can it truly be an effective standard? Also, if the standard for morals changes, then truth changes and the possibility for absolute truth goes out the window. Therefore, the finite godist has problems answering questions about the origin of God, the foundation for ethics, and the possibility for absolute truth.

Theism (a.k.a. monotheism)

Examination—Monotheism, the belief that there is one infinite being, is often simply called "theism." Theism defends the notion that God is an ultimately perfect being who wants to have a relationship with his creation. His perfection extends to every area of his being: his knowledge, power, presence, and goodness. Because of his perfection, he cannot change, for to change something that is perfect only results in imperfection. God's immutability is readily found in scripture, most blatantly in Malachi 3:6, "I

[15] John Stuart Mill, *Autobiography*, 1873, ch. 2, electronic text can be found at: http://socserv2.socsci.mcmaster.ca/~econ/ugcm/3ll3/mill/auto.

[16] On the openness of God movement see Greg Boyd's *Trinity and Process* and *God of the Possible*, or Clark Pinnock's *The Openness of God*.

the Lord do not change."[17] For us, change is usually a good thing. Each can become a better person by learning or becoming stronger or more skilled. But for God, change in his nature would actually be an imperfection.

Secondly, let's revisit the "eight of life's most meaningful questions" from the beginning of the chapter.

1. Is there a God or any supernatural being? (Theology)
2. What is real? Is reality real? (Metaphysics)
3. What are the origins of man and the universe? (Cosmogony)
4. What is my meaning and purpose in life? (Teleology)
5. How do I know what is right and wrong? (Ethics, Axiology and Morality)
6. What is my destiny after death? (Eschatology and Immortality)
7. What is truth? How can I know it? (Epistemology)
8. What is the state of man? Is he good or sinful? (Anthropology)

The first thing to consider is whether or not Christian theism has an answer for each of these questions. Have you been taught about each of these answers? Two of these questions, numbers two and seven, have already been considered in this book. Number one was briefly mentioned in this chapter and will continue in the next. Question 5, ethics and morality, will be dealt with in chapter 12. The fact of the matter is that if a person takes an honest look at theism, it answers all of life's most meaningful questions without contradiction. You can know how things came into existence, who God is, where you will go when you die, and even your purpose in life if you commit yourself to a Christian worldview. Of course, this is not a knockdown argument, but you must realize as a Christian that you are able to answer questions about which other worldviews cannot even speculate. How can an atheist truly know that what he is doing is right or wrong? How can a polytheist know how his gods and the universe were created? They simply cannot know these answers while looking through the lens of their worldview.

This belief in theism is not exclusively "Christian." Two other major religions, Judaism and Islam, claim monotheism. It should be noted that while these other theistic religions may answer the questions above a little differently, they still have credible answers for life's most meaningful questions.

You will notice that there is no "critique" section here, but this is not due to the fact that there are no critiques of theism. This lack of critique is

---

[17] See also Jas. 1:17 and Ps. 102:25–27.

not a ploy to make our view look perfect and others unbelievable. Realize that three of the following chapters will deal with complaints against Christianity. Just like any other strategist, it is of utmost importance for the apologist to recognize the seemingly weak points in order to be prepared to defend against an attack. These supposed problems in Christian Theism usually revolve around the problem of evil, disagreements on our proofs for God, the Bible, the Trinity, and Christ's divinity.

Summary

The importance and understanding of each of these worldviews is crucial to an understanding of the religious and philosophical beliefs of the secular world around us. Memorizing these categories, as well as their critiques, will help in your encounter with each person with whom you come into contact. For instance, let's suggest that you begin a discussion with a person at lunch and he begins to wonder why it is that God must be omnibenevolent. They may claim "What if God is evil and he is just playing with us for fun?" Can you tell which worldview that this person is considering? During the discussion you hopefully recognized that this person was toying with the possibility that God is finite. If their idea is correct then God would be limited in regards to his goodness. In realizing that the person is arguing for finite godism, you could begin to interject critiques that were mentioned in the section on finite godism. Thus you may want to ask a question concerning ethics, "How could you know what is 'good' or 'evil' unless you have a perfect standard by which to measure?" In other words, how could he know God is evil unless there is a perfect standard to which he is comparing God? If this standard isn't God, then what is it?

Knowing what someone believes about the "eight of life's most meaningful questions" should lead us to understand his worldview as well. So, if a person tells you that there is no purpose in life and that everything "comes about by chance," it is very likely that the person subscribes to one of the two forms of naturalism. Again, if you know the worldview and the critiques against that view, then you will know what questions to lovingly ask. Notice that you have been encouraged to ask lots of questions. The goal here is to let the person find the truth for themselves. Oftentimes people feel that they are "preached to" by Christians. Yet if you ask them thought provoking questions, and the questions themselves expose the problems with the worldview, then they have to search for the answer while not feeling that you are forcing your beliefs on them. It is quite possible that they may ask your opinion, yet then they are requesting that you give your perspective and it appears much less forced.

While it may be impossible to prove that Christianity is 100% true, it is less difficult to give reasonable proof that theism is accurate. I don't think anyone could say that theism is easily demonstrable, but I think you might agree that the problems that infect the other worldviews and the consistency of theism, makes it the most attractive and reasonable of the bunch. The next chapter will prepare you to give evidence that God does in fact exist, and to point out some common objections to the arguments.

Study Questions

1. In your own words, explain what a worldview is.
2. What is the difference between an atheist and an agnostic? Make sure to mention "burden of proof" in your answer.
3. What is the difference between a benign and malignant agnostic?
4. Make a chart listing the seven different worldviews complete with a one-sentence description and a brief critique.
5. Do you think it is possible for a person to consistently and accurately hold to more than one worldview at a time?
6. Do you think it is possible for you, personally, to be able to critique other worldviews objectively, without letting your worldview get in the way?

Terms to Consider

Worldview
Naturalism
Atheism
Agnosticism
Supernaturalism
Finite/Infinite
Pantheism
Deism
Polytheism
Finite Godism
Theism

Memory Verse Options

Malachi 3:6

Going Beyond the Call of Duty: Readings for the Overachiever

Geisler, Norman, and William Watkins. *Worlds Apart: A Handbook on Worldviews*. Grand Rapids: Baker Books, 1989.

Nash, Ronald. *Faith and Reason: Searching for a Rational Faith*. Grand Rapids: Zondervan, 1988.

Naturalism
"There is nothing beyond the natural."

Atheism
"There is no god."

Agnosticism
"You can't know if there is a god."

Supernaturalism
"There is something beyond the natural."

Pantheism
"God and the World are identical."

Deism
"God exists, but he does not act in the universe."

Polytheism
"There are many finite gods."

Finite Godism
"God exists, but is limited in one or more aspects of his nature."

Monotheism
"There is one infinite and perfect being"

Chapter 7

Theism: Is It Credible?

"The existence of God, in so far as it is not self-evident to us, can be demonstrated from those of His effects which are known to us." [1]
—St. Thomas Aquinas

IN THIS chapter it will be shown that God's existence is demonstrable and the arguments for his existence are very convincing. Using the teleological, moral, and cosmological arguments, the basic proofs for God's existence will be considered. Similarly to the other chapters, there will be an examination of each argument as well as space given for a critique. While the critics have valid points, it will be shown that each of these three proofs for God's existence withstand the scrutiny of atheistic attacks.

The Credibility of Theism and the Possibility of Proving the Existence of God

Every time I have discussed the proofs for God's existence in a classroom setting, there has always been at least a hint of dissention among a couple of students. The following are the three most common objections to the proofs for God's existence.

1. "Our finite minds cannot comprehend the infinite essence of God, so it is impossible to prove he exists." While it is true that no one can know the infinite essence of God, this does not affect our knowledge of God's existence. The problem here is the person is confusing existence with essence. I would ask this person, "Do you have to know something completely in order to know that it exists?" If the answer was "yes," then this person could not know anyone or thing besides himself. How can you say that your best friend exists unless you know him completely? But to know someone completely is to know all their thoughts and past actions.

---

[1] Thomas Aquinas, *Summa Theologica*, I.2.2.

Is this possible? Therefore, you cannot claim to know the infinite essence of God, but you can argue that this infinite being exists.

2. "What is the point of proving God exists if I already believe in him?" Unfortunately, this person has missed an important goal of apologetics. Some of the things you are learning now may not be practical until you personally are in a crisis of belief or you discuss God with a troubled friend or a complete non-believer. While much of the focus in this book is on your personal faith and problems that may hinder your faith in college, never forget that it is our commission to help others find and accept Christ as their personal Lord and Savior. You may eventually meet an agnostic who has never heard of the proofs for God's existence. Maybe God will place you in a conversation that will leave the listeners wondering, "Maybe there are good reasons to believe that God exists!"

3. "We simply cannot prove the existence of a supernatural being." The usual response I give to this question is to formally demonstrate one of these arguments for God's existence. As long as you can present a logically sound argument with valid premises and a conclusion that ends with "God exists," then you have given solid evidence for the existence of God. I usually let the person who made this claim play "devil's advocate" to try and refute the argument. If the argument is irrefutable, then it is a logical proof for God's existence.

Three Arguments for God's Existence

There are many, many proofs for God's existence. The following paragraphs focus on three of the most popular and straightforward arguments that you can use to prove that God exists. Before lunging into rational fisticuffs, there are a few principles that must be contemplated.

First of all, the three arguments that will be examined are all *a posteriori* arguments. In other words, each of these three logical demonstrations deal with looking at the world and determining that the evidence presented by our senses results in the conclusion that God exists. It may be noticed that this is actually a very scientific endeavor. The scientific method will not be used, but rather, **forensic science** will be our method of demonstrating the existence of God. Due to the resurgence of forensic science used in modern crime and law oriented television shows, you are probably quite familiar with this field of study. In forensic crime investigations, detectives try to discover what caused an event or series of events to occur. They make conclusions based on the effects, or evidence, of the cause. If a man is found shot, the detectives attempt to determine who caused the shooting. They may take fingerprints, do analysis of the bullet, or find DNA evidence, along with many other investigative techniques. The investigators were not present at the moment the crime was committed. All they have to consider are the effects of the event. Christians are in the same boat. Christians must look at the world and argue that only God could have caused the effects that are seen in this world.

In order to understand these "effects" found in the world you must understand the concept of **necessary conditions.** A necessary condition is simply a prerequisite that must be obtained before an event has the possibility of occurring. For example, there are four main conditions for a campfire to occur: matches, a lighter or something to start the fire with, something to burn, oxygen, and a person to produce the actual campfire. These are all necessary conditions. Without any one of these circumstances, a campfire will not occur. Suppose that you were walking through the woods and noticed that there was a campfire ahead; what could you assume without any further investigation? You could assume that each of the necessary conditions above was met. You would already know, without examination, that there was a person that started the fire, that some lighting device was used, that the presence of oxygen was evident, and that something was being burned.

As was stated above, necessary conditions are often used in reference to forensic science. Let's suggest that your class is invited to a murder mystery dinner theater where someone gets "killed" during the evening and you have to figure out who the murderer is. After dinner everyone is in the dining hall enjoying dessert. The doors and windows to the room are shut and locked. The lights go off and a shot rings out. The lights go up and one of your fellow students was "shot." Now there are a few things you can assume based merely on necessary conditions. The first thing you can assume, if there are no bullet holes in the windows, walls, or doors, is that someone inside that room was responsible for the shooting. The second thing you can assume is that someone in that room had used some sort of gun and it was still in the room. You may not think that this is much, but it should be pointed out that you have proven that a specific thing, "a gun," is present in the room without ever seeing the gun! In the same way that a worm-shaped hole in your apple proves that there was once a worm there, you can prove that God exists based on his effects and without ever actually seeing him!

The three arguments for God's existence that will be explained below will follow this same line of reasoning. In short, the teleological argument contends that if there is a design to the world then there must be a designer. The moral argument argues that if there is an objective moral law in this world then there must be a lawgiver. The cosmological argument states that if there is a finite world then there must be an infinite creator. For each of these proofs, premises must be defended: the world has design, there is a moral law present, and the world is finite. It also must be shown that the logic is coherent and each argument is logically sound. If, for each of these arguments, it is proven that the logic is sound and that the premises of the argument are true, then the result are reasonable proofs for God's existence.

The Teleological Argument

Examination—The word teleological comes from the Greek word *telos* simply meaning design or purpose. The teleological argument logically follows:

> If there is a design to the world, then there must be a designer.
> There is design to the world.
> Therefore, there must be a designer.[2]

William Paley, an eighteenth century theologian and philosopher, made the "watch in the forest" analogy famous. An excerpt here from Paley's *Natural Theology* will shed light on this argument:

> In crossing a heath, suppose I pitched my foot against a stone, and were asked how the stone came to be there, I might possibly answer, that, for anything I knew to the contrary, it had lain there for ever; nor would it, perhaps, be very easy to show the absurdity of this answer. But suppose I had found a watch upon the ground, and it should be inquired how the watch happened to be in that place, I should hardly think of the answer which I had before given, that, for any thing I knew, the watch might have always been there. Yet why should not this answer serve for the watch as well as for the stone? Why is it not as admissible in the second case as in the first? For this reason, and for no other, viz., that, when we come to inspect the watch, we perceive (what we could not discover in the stone) that its several parts are framed and put together for a purpose, e.g., that they are so formed and adjusted as to produce motion, and that motion so regulated as to point out the hour of the day; that, if the different parts had been differently shaped from what they are, of a different size from what they are, or placed after any other manner, or in any other order, than that in which

---

[2] Affirming the antecedent.

they are placed, either no motion at all would have been carried on in the machine, or none which would have answered the use that is now served by it . . . it requires indeed an examination of the instrument, and perhaps some previous knowledge of the subject, to perceive and understand it; but, being once, as we have said, observed and understood) the inference, we think, is inevitable, that the watch must have had a maker: that there must have existed, at some time, and at some place or other, an artificer or artificers who formed it for the purpose which we find it actually to answer; who comprehended its construction, and designed its use.[3]

Paley's main contention was simply that if a watch needs a designer, how much more does our universe need an intelligent mind for its apparent design. If, in our experience, only intelligent beings create structured objects, then why should it be different with the material world? Shouldn't it be logical for us to propose that some higher intelligent being exists?

Critique—Of course, the naturalist disagrees; yet notice that there is only one other option: everything came about by chance. The naturalist generally does not argue the logic of the teleological argument, but rather denies one of the premises. He doesn't reject the minor premise simply due to the fact that there is not a commonsensical man on earth who denies that the world is "ordered," or that it has some structure. For without this structure the planets would simply fly out of orbit and our molecular makeup would vanish into thin air. Instead, the naturalist denies the major premise in the argument above. The atheist disagrees that this order demands a designer.

There are two ways to look at this concept of "chance" as a possible evasion of the notion of a God. Let's suggest that when you arrive home from today's events, you open your door to an interesting sight. Immediately when you open the door, you see a winding chain of falling dominoes that stream throughout your entire house. They go through the bedrooms, upstairs, onto the kitchen countertop, everywhere! After viewing this experience you immediately figure out two *necessary conditions*. The first will be discussed in our section on the cosmological argument, and that is simply that someone had to knock over the first domino. The second is that someone came into your house and set up these dominoes. Never in history has anyone seen dominoes that set themselves up, nor has anyone observed any event that has ordered a pile of dominoes into an upright and single file position without the use of an intelligent mind.

---

[3] William Paley, *Natural Theology* (New York: Harper and Brothers, 1847), electronic text found at http://home.att.net/~p.caimi/Paley-Chap1.doc.

There is often a funny quote that creeps up when discussing the notion of chance, "If you have enough monkeys banging randomly on typewriters, they will eventually type a work of William Shakespeare." Ironically enough, a group of students from University of Plymouth in England proposed to investigate this claim. They set up a single computer in an exhibit with six primates. After a month, the BBC reported that the monkeys "had only succeeded in partially destroying the machine, using it as a lavatory, and mostly typing the letter 's'," and "failed to come up with anything that remotely resembled a word."[4] Likewise, there are a few internet sites that have hypothetically set millions of monkeys in motion in front of a typewriter, let trillions of years pass, and it still has only resulted in only a few words from a Shakespearean work. The possibility of monkeys typing a full work of any author, even Dr. Seuss, is irrational.

There are two things can be learned from this analogy. The first thing is that there is a big difference between dominoes and Shakespeare. Dominoes are not even close to the complexity needed to design our universe, one strand of DNA, or a momentous book. Dominoes are a simple design and Shakespeare is very complex. The chances of monkeys typing a work of Shakespeare are about the same as a full sentence randomly popping up in your alphabet soup. It seems to most that this complexity is too tough for chance theorists to explain.

Secondly, it must be pointed out that an abundance of time doesn't help the naturalist. Usually atheists, especially evolutionists, will argue that although you cannot see changes occurring at present, over billions of years order and structure occurs. This is simply incomprehensible; in fact, scientists have observed the exact opposite in reality. Nature appears to become disordered as time moves on. Norman Geisler explains:

> Simple observation reveals that if one drops bags of red, white, and blue confetti from an airplane a thousand feet above the ground it will not form an American flag on someone's lawn. The laws of nature, apart from intelligent intervention, will randomize the colors; they will not form fifty stars and thirteen stripes out of them. And both observation and experimentation demonstrate that dropping the colored paper fragments from ten thousand feet will not provide the necessary time for them to organize. There is only one cause known to human beings that can organize these tiny pieces of paper into an American flag, and that is intelligence.[5]

---

[4] BBC News, "No words to describe monkeys' play" published May 9, 2003, [INTERNET], http://news.bbc.co.uk/go/pr/fr/-/1/hi/england/devon/3013959.stm.

[5] Norman Geisler, *Baker encyclopedia of Christian apologetics*, 700.

Another complaint against the teleological argument is that it does not exclusively prove that the God of Christian theism exists; it also could be used to prove that a deistic god exists or even that polytheism is the true worldview. While this seems to be a valid critique, it seems that most are content to use the teleological argument to prove that some supernatural and intelligent being must exist. After this is established, then the theist can argue against deism and polytheism.

While it does seem that the teleological argument doesn't specifically prove the Christian Theistic worldview, the critique that design does not imply a designer is incredible. Scientists have never observed a random series of events produce ordered and structured objects. Thus you may conclude with clear rationale that there is a God who designed the material universe.

The Moral Argument

Examination—The Moral Law Argument stems from the truth that each one of us senses that there is a correct way that man ought to behave. The atheist, pantheist, and polytheist, are all aware that each of us has the potential to act correctly or incorrectly. The question that the moral argument asks is simply, "By what standard are we to judge these actions?" There are only two options: this standard is subjective to each individual or it is from an objective, external source. If someone claims that this standard is subjective and merely an opinion then it is not a standard at all! Each person would have different claims for what is right and wrong and this would result in relativism. The only other option is that there is an intelligent being as the source of the moral law. The argument in syllogistic form can be viewed:

> If there is an absolute moral law, then there must be a lawgiver.
> There is an absolute moral law.
> Therefore, there must be a lawgiver.[6]

The apologist who was the most vocal proponent of this argument was C. S. Lewis. He discusses in *Mere Christianity* the preference between moral systems. For instance, none of his readers would have suggested that the morality of the Nazis was better than the morality of the Judeo-Christian morality that is common today. He then shows how this proves that there must be an absolute moral law:

[6] Affirming the antecedent.

The moment you say that one set of moral ideas can be better than another, you are, in fact, measuring them both by a standard, saying that one of them conforms to that standard more nearly than the other. But the standard that measures two things is something different from either. You are, in fact, comparing them both with some Real Morality, admitting that there is such a thing as a real Right, independent of what people think, and that some people's ideas get nearer to that real Right than others.[7]

C. S. Lewis concludes that if, in any situation, a person claims that one act is "right" and another "wrong," then there must be an absolute moral law.

Critique—There seem to be only two possible ways for a non-believer to critique this argument. First, they could deny that an absolute moral law categorically implies that there is a lawmaker. Secondly, they could deny that there is an absolute moral law at all! Either of these objections, if substantiated, would render the moral law inept.

The first contention is that the absolute law that humanity lives by is not necessarily attributable to the presence of a lawgiver, but is more likely due to man's natural herd instinct or possibly just the culture or society in which one lives. But the moral law cannot be some sort of instinct due to the fact that sometimes humans commit good acts that deny our herd instinct. A good illustration of this is 9/11. When thousands of people were running away from danger, brave rescue workers were running into fatally burning buildings attempting to save trapped people. Their instincts told them to run away, but the right and even heroic thing to do was to run into a dangerous situation. Therefore, the moral law could not be herd instinct. Secondly, the moral law could not be due to merely the culture or society. It seems as though there are central moral tenets that stream through each of the world's great societies. For instance, selflessness is always seen as a good behavior and selfishness is always bad. Why is this the case? Because there is an absolute moral law that influences each of these cultures. You may be wondering, "What about horrible cultures like Nazi Germany?" The question itself proves the point. You know that the Nazi regime was evil, but why was it evil? In asking the question, you unknowingly imply that there is an objective moral standard by which to measure each culture.

The second critique revolves around the fact that there may not be an absolute moral law at all! If you remember our discussion on relativism,

---

[7] C. S. Lewis, *Mere Christianity* (New York: Simon and Schuster, 1996), 25.

the same rebuttal applies here as well. For, if there are no absolutes, then everything is an opinion. But when dealing with ethical issues people do not express opinion as much as they express absolutes. They say things like "He shouldn't have done that," and "Did you hear what Betty said the other day?" Each of these implies that the actions taken were in some way wrong and incorrect behavior. Again, what is the standard by which these actions are judged? If there is no standard and our words are mere opinion, then you have no right making the smallest judgment. C. S. Lewis comments on the problem, "Whenever you find a man who says he does not believe in a real Right and Wrong, you will find the same man going back on this a moment later. He may break his promise to you, but if you try breaking one to him he will be complaining 'It's not fair' before you can say Jack Robinson."[8] Lewis points out that when someone claims any judgment whatsoever, such as fairness, then a moral absolute has been assumed.

The moral law argument has successfully deflected the complaints of its detractors. A moral law does seem to exist, and thus, must have been established by an outside source. This external and objective source must be an intelligent being and not merely an object, for what object can create an ethical system? Therefore, the conclusion of the moral law argument is maintained; there is a transcendent moral lawgiver.

The Cosmological Argument

Examination—The word cosmological comes from the Greek word *cosmos* simply meaning world or universe. The argument asks the question, "How did the material universe get here?" The theist realizes that if this world is comprised of beings that are dependent on each other for their initial existence, then there must be an eternal, infinite being that grounds all of existence. In other words, there must be some uncaused cause that has caused everything else to exist.

The easiest way to comprehend this situation is to simply think of our parents, and their parents, whose parents had them and so forth. Could you theoretically go back in time and follow this historical line back to God's creation of Adam and Eve? Even if a person doesn't believe in Adam and Eve, could they find the first amoeba in the primordial stew? On the other hand, could someone argue that parents have been having kids forever, so that you cannot find the first cause of this line of humans? This ridiculous type of reasoning is what philosophers call an **infinite regress** of

---

[8] Ibid., 19.

causes. This simply means that the cause/effect scenario has been happening forever and it never had a given starting point.

> Part one of our Cosmological Argument is as follows:
> If an infinite regress is not possible,
> then there must be an infinite thing that grounds all existence.
> An infinite regress is not possible
> Therefore something infinite must exist.[9]

One of the strongest points of the cosmological argument is that very few people have ever agreed with the possibility of an infinite regress of causes. An infinite regress of causes is simply unacceptable. Our senses show and our reason exclaims that there must be a cause for every effect. This is the **principle of causality** in a nutshell: for every effect there must be a cause. Take for instance this situation: you arrive at a railroad crossing and you see the train cars go by. You did not see the engine, but you know that there must be one up there, because the cars are moving. The engine is a necessary condition for the cars to be moving. Remember the domino illustration in the teleological argument section? It also applies here. Someone or thing must cause that first domino to fall. Even if it were the wind, this thing is a necessary condition for falling dominoes to occur. By looking at the world full of causes and effects everyone should realize that there cannot be an infinite regress of causes. Thus there must be a thing which does not have a creator. This thing started the chain of events that has given us our present situation. This infinite thing is our necessary condition.

There Must Be Something Infinite

Notice that the word "God" has not even been used at this point. The message up to this point is simply that *there must be something infinite*. Nothing else would make sense! Take a look at the confusion in this statement by our friendly atheist, Bertrand Russell:

> When I was a young man and was debating these questions very seriously in my mind, I read John Stuart Mill's Autobiography, and I there found this sentence: "My father taught me that the question 'Who made me?' cannot be answered, since it immediately suggests the further question 'Who made God?' That very simple sentence showed me, as I still think, the fallacy in the argument of the First Cause. If everything must have a cause, then God must

[9] Affirming the antecedent.

have a cause. If there can be anything without a cause, it may just as well be the world as God, so that there cannot be any validity in that argument.[10]

There are two problems with Russell's logic here. First, he contends, "everything must have a cause." Note that some atheists claim that the principle of causality should read, "everything has a cause" instead of "every effect has a cause." If their version were true, it would be as ludicrous as claiming the possibility of an infinite regress. Russell was one of the few philosophers who argued that an infinite regress was actually possible.[11] While his ideas were counterintuitive and widely criticized, they helped Russell live with his contention that God need not exist.

Secondly, Russell mentions that the infinite thing "may just as well be the world as God." While Russell is not really claiming that the universe is infinite, he is simply arguing, "Why can't it be the world that is uncaused?" This brings us to the second part of the cosmological argument:

This infinite thing is either a being or the universe.
It cannot be the universe.
Therefore the infinite thing must be a being.[12]

Your first thought after reading this argument should have dealt with the critique leveled against pantheism in the last chapter. Pantheists consider that God is everything and is infinite. But of course, the world cannot be an infinite thing due to the fact that it changes and that it had a beginning. In this situation, when dealing with a person who is familiar with science, it would be advised that you bring up the Big Bang Theory. Mentioning this theory does not mean you believe in it, but you are simply using the atheist's scientific beliefs as an opportunity to prove your point. Most scientists at this point in history believe in some version of the Big Bang theory, therefore they know that there was a beginning to this vast universe. Thus they usually comprehend that the world cannot be infinite. But there are those who stubbornly disagree that a being must have created it. Here is a true threefold dilemma to present to the staunchest of atheists concerning the beginning of the universe:

1. The universe has always existed. The problem with this theory is that modern science seems to offer evidence to the contrary. For instance,

[10] Bertrand Russell, *Why I am not a Christian*, 6–7.

[11] See Bertrand Russell's *The Principles of Mathematics*, 2nd ed. (London: Allen and Unwin, 1937), 358–59. Or simply search the internet for the Tristram Shandy paradox.

[12] Denying an alternate.

Mark Eastman writes, "According to their calculations, time and space had a finite beginning that corresponded to the origin of matter and energy."[13] This is one of the conclusions of Einstein's law of relativity. Time, matter, and even space came into existence all at the same time! Einstein said in a lecture before the Prussian Academy of Sciences, January 27, 1921, "I must not fail to mention that a theoretical argument can be adduced in favor of the hypothesis of a *finite universe.*"

While scientists have their theories, philosophers have been debating this possibility for centuries. One of the best arguments against an infinite cosmos is the Kalam Cosmological argument. The foundation of this argument is the notion that you cannot add to an infinite. So when someone says "infinity plus one," then the statement is deemed an absurdity. But if this world is infinite and has been here forever, then we would have infinite moments in the past. Yet if moments are still happening and even the most precious milliseconds tick by, aren't we adding moments to an infinite? Thus philosophically, time itself cannot be infinite; it must have had a beginning.

2. It simply popped into existence. No one has ever seen an object "pop" into existence. This option should immediately throw up some red flags. Whenever you hear someone claim that some form of "quantum physics" or "random singularity" started the chain of events, then he is claiming that the universe popped into existence due to mere chance. Yet if nothing existed before the "Big Bang," how could something come from nothing? Could chance cause something to exist from nonexistence? Norman Geisler has some interesting thoughts on the matter: "Chance is only a statistical description of the likelihood of events. Only forces or powers can cause events. Chance merely describes the likelihood of a force (or forces) producing a given event. Chance cannot be a cause in terms of the cosmological argument. Chance is not a power, and a nonpower cannot cause anything."[14] This understanding of chance should help us combat the atheist's objections. Chance must always begin with an object already in existence. You can investigate the chance that dice will roll a certain number or the chances that your school baseball team will win the championship. Yet you cannot predict the chances of something coming from nothing. This would be like giving the chances that 1 plus 1 will equal 4. **Chance** is not a power, but is only a statistical consideration of already

[13] Mark Eastman and Chuck Missler, *The Creator: Beyond Time and Space* (Word for Today, 1996), 11.

[14] Norman Geisler, *Baker Encyclopedia of Christian Apologetics*, 293.

existing causes. Therefore one cannot claim "chance" caused something to come from nothing.

As a side note, realize that quantum theorists come up with new theories every day. The biggest problem with these theories is that they are unsubstantial. They are all attempting to base their conclusions on models and possibilities of what existed prior to the "Big Bang." Yet no one can know for sure what materials, if anything, existed before our universe came into existence. But remember, most modern physicists argue that *nothing* existed before the big bang!

While this option is quite absurd, you will actually find uneducated atheists trying to use this line of reasoning. Ask them what caused the big bang and they may begin to explain the dense ball of matter or the gasses that formed the matter, but what they are doing is stating that the universe created itself. What you have to continually ask is, "Where did the gasses come from?" Whatever element they claim started the universe, ask them where that thing originated. The fact of the matter is that an honest scientist will state that they simply don't know. They don't have any trustworthy scientific information about what existed before the beginning of the universe.

3. An infinite intelligent being created it. The famous NASA astronomer Robert Jastrow wrote, "For the scientist who has lived by his faith in the power of reason, the story ends in a bad dream. He has scaled the mountains of ignorance; he is about to conquer the highest peak; as he pulls himself over the final rock, he is greeted by a band of theologians who have been sitting there for centuries."[15] The only option left is that there is an infinite being who created this vast universe.

Critique—There have been a few critiques mentioned in the examination section; for instance, that an infinite series of causes is actually possible. Yet there are a few minor critiques that have been neglected. For instance, the existence of an "uncaused cause" or God, does not imply that this being is personal, loving, omnipotent, or any of God's other attributes. While there will be an argument against this point in the next paragraph, you should be reminded that it has already been shown that the infinite "thing" must be a being and cannot be the material world. In other words, no matter if this being is omnipotent or loving or not, it has been proven that *there is a being* that was not caused by any external force and who created the world. This seems to be a strong achievement in and of itself.

[15] Robert Jastrow, *God and the Astronomers* (New York: W.W. Norton and Company, 1978), 116.

This contention that an infinite being does not imply the other attributes of God is not sound. For example, it is very likely that a timeless creator is also omnipotent. If a being is found to be without cause then it is infinite in respect to time. So, in this respect, you can be sure that the being stated in the cosmological argument is infinite in at least one sense. He is the cause of everything in existence. If this infinite being has given existence to everything, which he created out of nothing, it seems logical to assume that he also has the power to manipulate or destroy his creation. Which seems to be the bigger feat: to turn nothing into something or to simply unorganize a set of molecules? For to destroy or manipulate his creation God only needs to move, not create. It seems that the power to create something out of nothing is the most powerful action that any being could perform. Therefore, it does not seem like such a logical jump to assume that a being that created out of nothing and was the cause of this material universe also has all the power needed to do whatever he would like!

These last few paragraphs showed that with some thought, you can demonstrate that it is plausible that a being that is infinite in relation to time seems to also denote a being that has other good qualities, namely omnipotence. While this position may not be demonstrable using pure logic, it appears that it is credible that a being that is infinite in respect to time also implies a much more complex being.

Summary

This chapter dealt with the three most popular and credible arguments for the existence of God. Each argument is an *a posteriori* argument: one that argues from effect to cause. The philosopher looks at the world and determines that God is a necessary condition for the effects in the universe to exist. In the teleological argument, we argue from design to designer. In the moral argument, we argue from absolute moral law to absolute moral lawgiver. Lastly, in the cosmological argument, we argue from a finite world to an infinite creator.

The study of the proofs for God's existence often lead down some deep and complex roads. Be prepared in class to discuss each of these three arguments and give your opinion. But most of all, if you are confused about any of these arguments, be ready to ask questions of your teacher and colleagues.

Study Questions

1. Why do some people think the arguments for God's existence are ineffective?
2. How can we use forensic science to prove that God exists?
3. Give your own example of a set of necessary conditions for a given event. (Do not use the example in the book (campfires.)
4. Out of the three arguments for God's existence, which do you find the most compelling? Why?
5. Present the three possibilities for how the universe began and, in your own words, discredit two of the options.
6. In the hypothetical statement below, what is the rule of logic used to describe this form of proof? (see "terms to consider" in chapter 5 if you need help)

   If there is an absolute moral law, then there must be a lawgiver.
   There is an absolute moral law.
   Therefore, there must be a lawgiver.

7. In the disjunctive statement below, what is the rule of logic used to describe this form of proof? (see "terms to consider" in chapter 5 if you need help)

   This infinite thing is either a being or the universe.
   It cannot be the universe.
   Therefore the infinite thing must be a being.

Terms to Consider

Forensic Science
Necessary Conditions
Teleological Argument
Moral Argument
Cosmological Argument
Infinite Regress
Principle of Causality
Chance

Memory Verse Options

Romans 1:20
Hebrews 11:6

Going Beyond the Call of Duty: Readings for the Overachiever

Craig, William Lane. *The Kalam Cosmological Argument*. Eugene, OR: Wipf and Stock Publishers, 1979.

Jastrow, Robert. *God and the Astronomers*. New York: W.W. Norton and Company, 1978.

Chapter 8

Charges Against Theism: Evil

"If an omnipotent, omnipresent, and omnibeneficent God is responsible for the world as we know it, then how [do Christians] explain evil?"[1]
—Paul Kurtz

An Introductory Analysis

ONE OF the greatest charges against classical theism is the presence of evil. While many Christians would claim that the presence of goodness in this world is a reflection of the almighty being, these same people get befuddled when an atheist claims that the evil that exists in this world reveals to us that God cannot be perfect. Some even state that if God exists, then he must be evil.

As a side note, it should be pointed out that sometimes when a person has problems with the evil in this world it may not be caused by an intellectual problem. While they may say that because of evil, they don't believe in God, it may be a more complicated issue. Sometimes you may talk to a person that has had such horrible things happen to them during their lifetime that they blame God for their misfortunes. This anger sometimes manifests itself into a complete abandonment of the idea that God exists.

If you have ever seen the movie *Forrest Gump* you may remember a character in the movie named Lieutenant Dan. Dan had lost his legs in the Vietnam War; a war in which he would have died if it hadn't been for Forrest's valiant efforts to save him. Yet Dan was remorseful; he would have rather died honorably in battle than to live a tough life without legs. At one point in the movie while on their shrimp boat in a storm, Dan had a verbal confrontation with God. The movie doesn't go into detail, but it is

[1] Paul Kurtz, "Why I Am a Skeptic about Religious Claims," originally in *Free Inquiry* magazine, used here from http://www.secularhumanism.org/index.php?section=library&page=pkurtz_26_4.

stated the next day that Dan "made his peace with God." The point of this section is that you need to be aware that sometimes the problem of evil can go much deeper than your opponent actually reveals. The individual may actually be asking, "Why did God let this happen to me?" As with the case of Job in the Old Testament, the answer may not be promptly given by God. If God does not answer, then of course, no one is able to give a definitive answer. Sure, Christians may suggest that God has a purpose in allowing evil, but sometimes this pill is hard to swallow, especially if unfortunate events have occurred recently. In these sorts of situations, you can usually only help console and pray for this hurt individual.

The Philosophical Problem of Evil

Laying the sympathetic gestures aside, the **problem of evil** is one of the greatest critiques ever leveled against the theistic religions of the world. The argument is simply this: If God is all-good (**omnibenevolent**), all-knowing (**omniscient**) and all-powerful (**omnipotent**), then why does evil exist? If God wants the best for us, and has the power to give us the best world, then why doesn't he do it? For the theist, there is no doubt that God could wipe out Satan and his minions with a swoop of his proverbial hand. Those who argue that evil is an insurmountable problem simply ask, "Why doesn't he?" In hypothetical form, the argument goes as follows:

> If God existed as an omnipotent, omnibenevolent, and omniscient being, then evil cannot exist in his creation.
> Evil does exist in his creation.
> Therefore, God does not exist as an omnipotent, omnibenevolent, and omniscient being.

Here is how the argument works in the mind of the non-believer: if God isn't omnipotent, then he might not have the power to destroy the evil in this world. If God isn't omniscient, he may not know of certain evil acts that were taking place in the world, and thus, would not eliminate them. And if God isn't omnibenevolent then he does not always seek the perfect good of his creatures, so evil could exist. The atheist claims that at least one of these three attributes must be missing in God for the presence of evil in the world to make sense.

First, you may have noticed that the problem of evil is not a perfect argument for the non-existence of God. In other words, the argument does not prove explicitly that God does not exist. But don't be too excited for the problem is capable of destroying at least one of these three essential attributes of the creator: omniscience, omnipotence, or omnibenevolence. Take into account that these attributes are essential to the character of the Christian God. In fact, most theologians would claim that if you destroy one attribute of God, then the rest will follow. Here are some implications: If God is not all-powerful, he cannot control his own creation and has the possibility of being overtaken or even destroyed by one of his creatures. If God is not omniscient, then he does not have all knowledge and is susceptible to surprises and misfortunes. If God is not omnibenevolent, then God has the potential to do evil. Eliminating just one attribute of God renders God a finite being and not the God of Christianity.

There are only two ways to combat the argument stated above. First, you could deny one of the premises; or secondly, you could deny the logic being used. Before reading on, examine the logic of the syllogism above. Is the logic valid? The argument is presented in the logical form "denying the consequent," which is accurate and logically sound. Since this option is illegitimate, then look at each of the two premises to see if you disagree with either. Any orthodox Christian would not deny the second premise, "Evil does exist in his creation," so the first premise is where you should turn your attention. Does it necessarily follow that if God is omnipotent, omniscient, and omnibenevolent, then evil would not exist in his creation? The answer to this question will be the subject of the rest of this chapter.

An Examination of Evil

It is true that many Christians struggle with the concept of the existence of evil. Recently, I was approached by a workman at school and was told that he and his colleagues had recently discussed the question: "Did God create evil?" The problem they encountered was this: If God created everything, then didn't he create evil as well? If God were an omnibenevolent God, why would he create evil?

The solution to this problem lays in the word "everything." The fact of the matter is that sin is not a "thing." It is actually the lack of a thing. **Sin** in general is the state where a given thing is missing what it is expected and designed to have.[2] The word *sin* comes from the ancient sport of archery. When archers would miss the bull's-eye, they would say the word "sin." They could shoot very close to perfect, but even if they missed the mark by a millimeter, it was still called sin. The archers expected them-

---

[2] Usually when you think of sin, you think of inappropriate actions and offensive behavior. This is a specific type of sin: moral sin. When the word sin is used in this chapter the focus is not specifically on moral sin, but rather, all types of imperfections.

selves to be perfect. Thus, any sort of imperfection is, in the general sense of the word, sin.

St. Thomas Aquinas stated, "Evil is simply a privation of something which a subject is entitled by its origin to possess and which it ought to have, as we have said. Such is the meaning of the word 'evil' among men. Now, privation is not an essence; it is, rather, a negation in a substance."[3] Aquinas uses the word **privation** here to describe evil. In other words, when something is deprived of what it was given by the creator, then in this regards, it is evil. You see, evil is like a hole in a bucket. It's simply something missing that the thing is expected to have. Therefore, a chair that is missing a leg is evil. A car without an engine is evil and a human who performs actions not intended by the perfect creator is also evil.

With this definition in mind, is it possible for something to be completely evil? No! If something is completely deprived of "good" then it doesn't even exist! If existence is something "good," then to be completely deprived of "good" is to be non-existent. A good analogy of sin is rot that destroys trees and rust that destroys automobiles. Can you have a fully rotten tree or a fully rusted car? There comes a point where the tree no longer is a tree, and a car becomes a pile of rust and can no longer be called an automobile. Or, back to the bucket analogy, can you have a completely "holed" bucket? If so, you would be carrying around a handle! Thus, in the same way, you cannot have a fully evil entity. Even Satan is not completely evil! He does have a few good qualities. For instance, Satan is a very intelligent strategist. He knows how to disrupt and annoy God's people so that they are not effective in God's work. He is also said to be a beautiful angel of light.[4] But beauty is a quality that God possesses as well! Therefore, a thing cannot remain itself and be completely evil.

There are two points to consider after reading this section. First, notice that our initial problem has been taken care of due to the fact that evil is not a "thing" to be created. Evil is a privation of a thing. Therefore, God, our omnibenevolent creator, did not create evil! God created a perfect world, but then it was messed up by his own creation. In fact, you cannot even say, "Humanity created evil." Evil isn't a "thing" to be created, it is a privation of a good thing.[5] But rather, man perverted what was good and what the creator intended. Once humanity had tainted his creation, then the imperfection that was evident was called "evil."

[3] Thomas Aquinas, *Summa Contra Gentiles*, 3.7.2.

[4] 2 Cor. 11:14.

[5] Remember, if evil is a "thing," then God must have created it. He created every*thing!*

The second point considers another question that is crucial to up-holding God's omnibenevolence and omnipotence: "Why did God allow evil to happen?" For if God is all-powerful, couldn't God have created a place where we wouldn't have done evil? While it seems that the first bullet has been dodged, another one follows seeking to destroy one of God's attributes. Consequently, the debate must continue.

Why did God Allow Evil to Happen?

This section and the one that follows consider why an omnipotent God would allow evil to occur in his perfect creation. It seems natural to humans that if one of us creates something, whether it be as simple as a finger-painting or as complex as a building, the good thing to do would be to protect that creation from perversion and destruction. A child puts its finger-painting on the refrigerator and keeps his siblings from ripping it down and desecrating it. The architect takes every step to ensure that his skyscraper will be able to resist the harshest of elements and, unfortunately in this day and age, be able to take on anything that a terrorist throws at it. So, in light of these things, the question of God's protective power does come into question. Why did God allow Adam and Eve to eat of the apple? Even further in the past, why did God allow Lucifer to rebel?

The solution to the problem lies in the doctrine of free will. Norman Geisler summarizes the thought of Aquinas and Augustine in five points:

1. God is absolutely perfect.
2. God created only perfect creatures.
3. One of the perfections God gave some of his creatures was the power of free choice.
4. Some of these creatures freely chose to do evil.
5. Therefore, a perfect creature caused evil.[6]

The focus of these five points should be on sentence number three. If it is posited that God has given us free choice, how is it possible that he could make certain choices on our behalf? Take for instance any situation where a decision between right and wrong must be made. If man did not have free will, an omnibenevolent God would have to choose the right choice for us. Therefore it seems that God only had two choices when he created: create a world with beings with free will and the possibility of evil, or create a deterministic world where agents would not have true free choice and God would make the choices for them.

[6] Norman Geisler, *Baker encyclopedia of Christian Apologetics*, 219.

C. S. Lewis in his *Mere Christianity* beautifully illustrates this point:

> God created things which had free will. That means creatures which can go either wrong or right. Some people think they can imagine a creature which was free but had no possibility of going wrong; I cannot. If a thing is free to be good it is also free to be bad. And free will is what has made evil possible. Why, then, did God give them free will? Because free will, though it makes evil possible, is also the only thing that makes possible any love or goodness or joy worth having. A world of automata—of creatures that worked like machines—would hardly be worth creating. The happiness which God designs for His higher creatures is the happiness of being freely, voluntarily united to Him and to each other in an ecstasy of love and delight compared with which the most rapturous love between a man and a woman on this earth is mere milk and water. And for that they must be free.[7]

In addition, it should be pointed out that evil sometimes is merely an accidental byproduct of good, and not necessarily a choice. Sometimes accidents happen where evil occurs unintentionally. Due to the free world you live in, humans can make good free choices that result in evil effects. For instance, if your parents decide to go out to eat, which is good, and get in a car accident and are injured, then this is evil that resulted from a good act. In another example, the blacksmith's hammering produces sparks that burn down his workshop. The blacksmith's act of creation was a good action, but it unintentionally sparked evil. Therefore, sometimes evil is not a choice but an unintentional byproduct of good.

While it can be agreed that evil is an unfortunate by-product of our free will, whether intentional or not, one may wonder if God still does bear some of the responsibility for the existence of evil. There is no doubt that the situation in which man finds himself is his own fault and not the fault of the almighty being, yet can God be somewhat to blame? While it is true that God has allowed the possibility of evil to exist, humans are the ones who actually commit the evil act. Therefore, can man blame God for even allowing the possibility of evil? I don't think it will be denied that God's responsibility was to create the most perfect world possible. It seemed to Him, and luckily for us, that to create a world of free creatures would be better than one comprised solely of robots. Therefore, do we have a right to blame God for his blessing to us and our own failure as free creatures? This blame does not seem to be morally proper nor intellectually sound.

[7] C. S. Lewis, *Mere Christianity*, 52–53.

Why does God Still Allow Evil to Happen?

While it may seem that the origin of evil has been dealt with, the question still remains about the current state of affairs. Why doesn't he destroy evil now? If God is all-powerful, couldn't he wipe out evil in the present?

First, the frightening implications of this argument should be observed before you take this question seriously. For if all evil was destroyed, and humanity is full of evil and sinful beings, wouldn't this entail the elimination of humanity? For all of us have "sinned and fall short of the glory of God."[8] Now of course, Christians believe there will be a judgment day that will result in a place full of believers whom God has perfected and who will live eternally with Him. You and I believe that God will eventually take care of evil and sin, but this has not happened yet. The point is that this event will take place, but only in God's timing and not mans'.

Secondly, it should be pointed out that evil does serve a purpose in God's plan. In some situations a greater good may not be possible without the chance of evil. Consider the qualities of bravery and sacrifice. Neither of these higher moral qualities would be possible without evil. For bravery to occur the firefighter must have a fire and the warrior must have a wicked opponent. For sacrifice to happen there must be a villain to commit the killing of the sacrificial lamb. Remember the words of Paul in Romans 5:3–4, "but we also rejoice in our sufferings, because we know that suffering produces perseverance; perseverance, character; and character, hope." Yet if there was no evil, could man learn perseverance? Could our character be developed to its potential without suffering? While evil is inherently reprehensible, it has been demonstrated that it does have some beneficial features that cannot be simply disregarded. Therefore, God does have a purpose for the presence of evil in our lives at the present time.

Revisiting the Moral Argument

On a last note, it should be pointed out that this argument against theism, the problem of evil, can be flipped on its head to be an argument for the existence of God. If you remember back to the last chapter, the moral argument asserted that if, in any situation, a person could claim that one act would be "right" and another "wrong," then there must be an absolute moral law. If there is an absolute moral law, then there must be a lawgiver. Therefore, if an atheist presents the problem of evil, he is already asserting that there is an absolute moral law. For to assert that something is evil, the

---

[8] Rom. 3:23.

atheist is implicitly asserting that there is a moral standard by which to determine what actions are good and which are bad. Thereafter, you can ask the atheist, "By what standard are you using to say that one action is evil and another is good?" The atheist is caught in a predicament. If he answers that there is no standard, then there is no such thing as "evil," thus disrupting his argument before it even has the chance to get off the ground. Yet if he says that there is an absolute standard of good and evil, you need to ask him who created that standard.

Summary

The problem of evil has plagued many ardent believers and has fueled the debates of atheists all around the world. In this chapter it was concluded that God did not create evil; in fact, evil is not a thing to be created. Evil, specifically known as "sin," is the lack of a thing, a privation, and a perversion of good. Therefore, God cannot be charged with "creating" evil. Evil happened when creatures chose to pervert the creator's intentions.

The main problem in this chapter revolved around God's ability to allow evil to exist in our world. The main question that needed to be addressed was, "Does it necessarily follow that if God is omnipotent, omniscient, and omnibenevolent, then evil would not exist in his creation?" The answer to this question is a resounding NO! The omnibenevolent God of theism decided that creating creatures with free will was a greater good than creating robots. If this option is presented to an atheist, he will undoubtedly agree. At this point in time when freedom and democracy prevail, there is no doubt that most people agree that freedom is better than being controlled by another. Unfortunately, with the ability to have free choice also comes the possibility of evil. God's power actually does not come into play in our scenario due to the fact that it is not logically possible to create a world of forced freedom, where God chooses that man acts freely good. This is a logical absurdity. God had the power to create a free world with the possibility of evil, or a world where he determined that everyone did only good acts. His choice to create the first option was determined to be the greater good.

Due to the fact that man is the cause of the evil in this world, God is not to blame for the existence of evil, although our opponents might charge that God should be blamed with creating a world with the potential of evil. Nevertheless, the creatures are the chief cause of evil; and humans, not God, should be to blame for our state of affairs.

Study Questions

1. Have you ever experienced a time in your life when you questioned the existence of God due to tragic events that occurred in your life? If comfortable, explain.
2. In your own words, explain the problem of evil.
3. Explain how the problem of evil, if not defended, could destroy God's omniscience, omnibenevolence, and his omnipotence.
4. Answer the questions, "Did God create evil?" and "Did man create evil?"
5. Why do you think God allowed evil to occur? How does your answer affect God's attributes?
6. How can the problem of evil be turned into an effective version of the moral argument?

Terms to Consider

Problem of Evil
Omnibenevolent
Omniscient
Omnipotent
Sin
Privation

Memory Verse Options

Ephesians 6:12
Romans 3:23

Going Beyond the Call of Duty: Readings for the Overachiever

Aquinas, Thomas. *Summa Contra Gentiles.* Notre Dame: University of Notre Dame Press, 1975.
Lewis, C. S. *A Grief Observed.* New York: Bantam, 1976.
———. *The Problem of Pain.* New York: Simon and Schuster, 1996.

Chapter 9

The Historicity of Christianity:
The Existence of Jesus

"Historically it is quite doubtful whether Christ ever existed at all,
and if he did we do not know anything about him."[1]
—Bertrand Russell

The Historicity of Christianity

ONE OF the first and foremost proofs for Christianity is substantiating its claim that it is indeed grounded in history. It is easy enough to presume that if Jesus never existed and that he was never crucified on a cross for our sins, then our religion does not have a foundation on which to build its doctrine. If Jesus doesn't exist, then there is no fellowship with the Father, no intercessory prayer in Jesus' name, and most importantly, no salvation by faith. How can faith be effective if our hope is based on a myth?[2] Therefore, over the next few chapters it will be shown that there is sufficient historical evidence that Jesus did exist and that the events portrayed in the Bible are historically accurate.

Objections from Skeptics

A quick perusal of the Internet while searching for "Jesus Myth" will result in finding that the belief that Jesus never existed is thriving among contemporary freethinkers. Most of these skeptics believe that Jesus is a mythological figure invented by first-century Jews. Timothy Freke and Peter Gandy have gained notoriety writing books that assert that Jesus is merely a myth: "For the original Christians, the Jesus story was a myth used to introduce beginners to the spiritual path."[3] These two writers have

---

[1] Bertrand Russell, *Why I am Not a Christian*, 11.

[2] 2 Pet. 1:16.

[3] Timothy Freke and Peter Gandy, *Jesus and the Lost Goddess* (New York: Random House,

become "convinced that the story of Jesus is not the biography of an historical Messiah, but a myth based on perennial Pagan stories."[4]

Those who are skeptical about Christianity occasionally mention that the historical "proof" for the existence of Christ is usually based on the Biblical account and is therefore biased and unusable. While the issue of Biblical authority will be defended in the next chapter, the paragraphs that follow will use *non-Christian sources* to prove that Jesus actually existed.

An Introduction to Examining Source Material

Before searching through these first and second century texts for evidence of Jesus' existence, you probably should examine your expectations. Sometimes young historians don't recognize the historical distance that spans between our world and the events in question. This may lead a person to falsely assume that our culture and technology is the same as when the events took place. This is an obvious fact: there were no mass media nor Internet technology that helped people communicate around the world. All they had was pen and parchment, a technique of communication that does not usually last for centuries. Also, people did not see Jesus as the "superstar" that he is today. The fact of the matter is that Jesus was the leader of a band of followers for three years and was rejected and ignored by many of those who heard his message. It wasn't until after he rose from the dead that his followers began to explode in number and have the huge impact on the 1st and 2nd century landscape. So, how much historical data should you expect to find?

The reason why this preface is written is due to the fact that recently it has been charged that there are no historical writings referring to Jesus written by an author who lived during Jesus' lifetime. While the atheist who made these charges completely and intentionally ignored the accounts of the gospels, he did ask a question Christians need to be able to answer, "Do we need to have historical writings from during Jesus' lifetime to prove our point?"

It does not seem, nor is it probable, that anyone will find any accounts of Jesus by a non-Christian historian that lived during his time period. But really, should archaeologists expect to find any writings by non-Christians during the lifetime of Jesus? Since the culture in which he lived rejected his teachings as heresy, it was unlikely that the Jews would

2001), 2.

[4] Timothy Freke and Peter Gandy, *The Jesus Mysteries* (New York: Three Rivers Press, 1999), 2.

write an early 1st century account of this would-be messiah. Do not be dismayed, there is a Jewish account of Jesus' trial and execution, but this was written at least 50 years later in the Jewish Talmud. On the other hand, the Romans were not overly concerned with Jesus until the Jews brought him to the attention of Pilate at the end of his ministry. You should not expect any historical evidence of Jesus from the Roman sector until after his death, which is exactly what is found in the words of Josephus and recorded in the paragraphs below.[5] The fact of the matter is that the atheist is asking for proof that likely does not, and should not exist. The atheist's expectations are far too extreme in this given situation.

To appease the atheist, let's find a cultural figure that lived during the time of Jesus and attempt to find historical sources that prove he existed. As a good comparison for the amount of information that should be found on Jesus, the existence of Tiberius Caesar Augustus will be questioned. Tiberius was the Roman Emperor during the time of Christ. To the Christian, there is no doubt that Tiberius existed; he is mentioned in the Bible. In the book of Luke the author mentions Tiberius to give his reader a timeline, "In the fifteenth year of the reign of Tiberius Caesar . . ."[6] Of course, since Tiberius reigned for twenty-three years, from 14-37 A.D., there should be many sources within 150 years of his life as compared to Jesus who only had a ministry of three years. Yet it may stun you to know that there are actually more non-Christian sources that discuss Jesus than the emperor Tiberius Caesar! Norman Geisler and Frank Turek write in their *I Don't Have Enough Faith to be an Atheist,* "There are ten known non-Christian writers who mention Jesus within 150 years of his life. By contrast, over the same 150 years, there are nine non-Christian sources who mention Tiberius Caesar, the Roman emperor at the time of Jesus."[7] Notice that this does not even count the Christian sources that talk about the life of Christ. If the Christian writers were added, the result would be a comparison of 43 sources for Christ to only 10 sources[8] for the Roman emperor![9]

With this in mind, it would seem that any historian who rejected the existence of Jesus would also have to reject the existence of this 1st century

[5] While it is possible to eventually find a letter by Pilate, they have yet to have found ANYTHING written by him.

[6] Luke 3:1.

[7] Norman Geisler and Frank Turek, *I Don't Have Enough Faith to be an Atheist* (Wheaton: Crossway Books, 2004), 222.

[8] The tenth source for Tiberius is the Luke passage mentioned above.

[9] Ibid., 222.

emperor. While it seems that the evidence is already in the Christian's favor, a brief look at the contents of some of these sources would be beneficial.

Non-Christian Sources

The first account, and one of the earliest historical reports, was from the Roman historian Tacitus. **Tacitus** was a writer and Roman administrator that lived from 55 A.D. to 120 A.D. One of his most famous works, *The Annals*, traces Roman history from 14 A.D. to 68 A.D. Tacitus is highly regarded as a very trustworthy Roman historian, and the contents of his *Annals* have not been explicitly criticized by modern scholarship. While the work was written around 109 A.D., it should be pointed out that Tacitus did live during the age of the eyewitnesses. While Tacitus never saw Jesus, he likely could have met people who had seen Jesus, possibly even Roman officials who were at Jesus' trial and crucifixion. Yet also, it can be speculated that Tacitus relied on Roman records to write his history. These records were very likely written very close to the time of Jesus. With this in mind, here is Tacitus' record of events:

> Nero . . . inflicted the most exquisite tortures on a class hated for their abominations, called Christians by the populace. *Christus, from whom the name had its origin, suffered the extreme penalty during the reign of Tiberius at the hands of one of our procurators, Pontius Pilatus*, and a most mischievous superstition, thus checked for the moment, again broke out not only in Judea, the first source of the evil, but even in Rome, where all things hideous and shameful from every part of the world find their center and become popular.[10]

Here is some of the information that can be deduced from this passage: A man by the name of Christus (Latin for Christ) lived during the time of Tiberius. Pontius Pilate was responsible for his death. He had followers who spread all over Judea and even into Rome. Nero tried to extinguish all of the Christians. Just in this single quote, there are four very important points of evidence concerning the history of Christianity.

Josephus was a Jewish man who lived from 37 A.D. to 97 A.D. He was actually born and named Joseph ben Matthias, but through a turn of events he was taken prisoner by the Roman General Vespasian and was renamed Flavius Josephus. He gained favor with Vespasian, helped the Romans understand the Jewish culture, and assisted with Roman/Jewish

---

[10] Tacitus, *Annals*, 15.44 (italics mine).

negotiations. After the Jewish war was over Josephus wrote a history of what he had seen and later wrote a book on the history of the Jews. This later book, *The Antiquities of the Jews,* chronicles Jewish history from creation to the recent conclusion of the Jewish Wars. The book, written around 93 A.D., is where Josephus discusses Jesus and his followers.

> At this time there was a wise man named Jesus. His conduct was good and [he] was known to be virtuous. And many people from among the Jews and the other nations became his disciples. Pilate condemned him to be crucified and to die. But those who became his disciples did not abandon his discipleship. They reported that he had appeared to them three days after his crucifixion, and that he was alive; accordingly he was perhaps the Messiah, concerning whom the prophets have recounted wonders.[11]

It should be pointed out that this citation has drawn criticism from Christian and non-Christian scholars alike. The version printed here is drawn from the Aramaic and is likely accurate, but the common Greek translation did not state that Jesus was "perhaps the Messiah," but rather "was the Messiah." It was very likely that Josephus, who worked for the Romans, would not claim, even if it were true, that he was a follower of Christ. Therefore, this translation of the Aramaic seems a much more credible report. On the acceptance of this source, there can be much more added to our list of historical evidence for Christ. Jesus was a wise man who was described by the populace as virtuous. Pilate crucified him. His disciples claimed that he appeared alive three days after his death and that he was the Messiah. Even if this specific source is not accepted, there is an indisputable quote from Josephus that reads, "Festus was now dead, and Albinus was but upon the road; so he assembled the Sanhedrim of judges, and brought before them the brother of Jesus, who was called Christ, whose name was James, and some others; and when he had formed an accusation against them as breakers of the law, he delivered them to be stoned."[12] Again, here is further evidence that Jesus existed, was called the Christ, and now here is evidence that he had a brother named James.

Suetonius, who was a Roman historian who lived from 69 A.D. to 140 A.D., wrote his work *The Lives of the Caesars* around 120 A.D. Here there is another mention of Christ, "As the Jews were making constant disturbances at the instigation of Chrestus, he [Claudius] expelled them from

[11] Josephus, *Antiquities of the Jews,* 18.3.3, cited in Geisler, *BECA,* 382.
[12] Ibid., 20.9.1.

Rome."[13] The purpose of the insertion of this quote is two-fold. First, and most obviously, here is another mention of Christ, although an interesting spelling, that comes within 100 years of his lifetime. Secondly, the event that this passage is describing is also mentioned in Acts 18:2, "There he met a Jew named Aquila, a native of Pontus, who had recently come from Italy with his wife Priscilla, because Claudius had ordered all the Jews to leave Rome." This event, which actually took place around 49 A.D., is another indication that the Biblical account corresponds to Roman history.

Pliny the Younger was the Roman governor of Bithynia, what is present-day Turkey. As one fairly new to the position of governor, the ruler constantly wrote letters to Emperor Trajan asking his advice on what to do in specific situations. Pliny was particularly puzzled with what to do with the Christians who had infected his population. The excerpt written around 112 A.D. gives insight into the mind of a troubled Roman official and the practices of early Christians:

> Meanwhile, in the case of those who were denounced to me as Christians, I have observed the following procedure: I interrogated these as to whether they were Christians; those who confessed I interrogated a second and a third time, threatening them with punishment; those who persisted I ordered executed . . . Those who denied that they were or had been Christians, when they invoked the gods in words dictated by me, offered prayer with incense and wine to your image, which I had ordered to be brought for this purpose together with statues of the gods, and moreover cursed Christ--none of which those who are really Christians, it is said, can be forced to do--these I thought should be discharged . . . [the Christians explained] that the sum and substance of their fault or error had been that they were accustomed to meet on a fixed day before dawn and sing responsively a hymn to Christ as to a god, and to bind themselves by oath, not to some crime, but not to commit fraud, theft, or adultery, not falsify their trust, nor to refuse to return a trust when called upon to do so.[14]

Pliny adequately describes how he dealt with those who admitted they were Christians, as well as what was necessary, in his eyes, to prove that they were no longer a part of the religion. What is most revealing is how Pliny describes the witness of the Christians. They worshiped Christ as if he were a God! In fact, Pliny understood that if a person were to worship a Roman god and pay homage to the image of the emperor, then they

[13] Suetonius, *Lives of the Caesars: Life of Claudius*, 25.4.
[14] Pliny the Younger, *Epp.* 10:96.

could be discounted as being a "Christian." While this excerpt does give evidence that Christ existed, its significance is based more on the theology of the early Christians. With this quote it can be determined that within 100 years of his death and resurrection, the followers of Christ believed in Jesus' divine nature.

The last source under the heading of non-Christian sources is the **Jewish Talmud**. The Babylonian Talmud, one of the two divisions of the work, was written over centuries by many scholarly Jews. The writing of this section of the Talmud likely commenced right after the destruction of the temple in 70 A.D., but the entire Talmud itself wasn't compiled until 200 A.D.[15] Unfortunately, it is not known when this section was written, yet you can be sure it was during the first or second century. The Talmud reads, "They hanged Yeshu [Jesus] on the Sabbath of the Passover. But for forty days before that a herald went in front of him (crying), 'Yeshu is to be stoned because he practiced sorcery and seduced Israel and lead them away from God. Anyone who can provide evidence on his behalf should come forward to defend him.' When, however, nothing favorable about him was found, he was hanged on the Sabbath of the Passover."[16] The text claims that Yeshua (the Hebrew form of Jesus) did exist and was killed on the eve of Passover.[17] It should be noted that the word "hanged" here refers to hanging on a cross, as mentioned in Galatians 3:13 and Deuteronomy 21:23.

Before moving on, notice that none of these writers had a reason to admit that Jesus existed. The Jews claimed that he was a blasphemer and Romans saw him as an instigator who riled up the Jewish nation. While neither of these two factions liked Jesus, they both agreed that he existed. But as an extra bonus they have given us some details of the life of Christ:

1. A man by the name of Christ lived during the time of Tiberius.
2. Jesus was a wise man who was described by the populace as virtuous.
3. He had a brother named James.
4. Pontius Pilate was responsible for his death.
5. He was killed on the eve of Passover.
6. The method of death was crucifixion.

[15] Geisler, *Baker Encyclopedia of Christian Apologetics*, 383.
[16] *The Jewish Talmud*, Sanhedrin 43a.
[17] This is mentioned in John 19:14.

7. His followers claimed that he appeared three days after his death, that he was the Messiah, and that he was God.
8. He had followers who spread all over Judea and even into Rome. [18]

Summary

While some liberal atheists continue to claim that Jesus never existed, it is without doubt that the historical evidence points to the contrary. There are ten credited sources written within 200 years of Jesus' life that state that Jesus did exist, as well as inform us about many other facts of his life.

Atheist historian Michael Grant was aware of the irrational conclusion of these liberal atheists. In his book, *Jesus: An Historian's Review of the Gospels*, he states:

> This skeptical way of thinking reached its culmination in the argument that Jesus as a human being never existed at all and is a myth . . . we can no more reject Jesus' existence than we can reject the existence of a mass of pagan personages whose reality as historical figures is never questioned . . . modern critical methods fail to support the Christ-myth theory. It has 'again and again been answered and annihilated by first-rank scholars.' In recent years, 'no serous scholar has ventured to postulate the non-historicity of Jesus'—or at any rate very few, and they have not succeeded in disposing of the much stronger, indeed very abundant, evidence to the contrary . . . .[19]

The testimony of Dr. Grant is no exception; it is actually the norm. Most history professors, no matter what worldview they embrace, deem that Jesus existed as well as accept the other facts acquired from these non-Christian sources. If confronted by an atheist who denies the existence of Jesus, first give all of the evidence presented in this chapter. If he still does not agree, challenge the atheist to find a few moderate historians with doctorates in their field to agree with his disbelief. If this person takes up this challenge, he will be sadly incapable of fulfilling it, and hopefully will recant his former position.

Unfortunately, some atheists fall into the same sort of bias of which they accuse Christians of committing. They have put rationality aside and ignored the historical evidence from non-Christian sources. At this point,

---

[18] Of the ten sources not examined in this section are Lucian, Thallus, Phlegon, Mara Bar-Serapion, and Celsus.

[19] Michael Grant, *An Historian's Review of the Gospels* (New York: Charles Scribners Sons, 1977), 199–200.

the Christian has exhausted all justifications necessary to adequately defend their position.

Yet isn't there much more to prove than simply the existence of Jesus? Of course, there is no mention of the salvation, the gospel message, or any other fundamental feature of the Christian faith in these non-Christian sources. The main source of these "essentials" is the Biblical accounts. Therefore, the next chapter will focus on defending the authority and historicity of the Bible.

Study Questions

1. Why is it important to be able to offer some people secular accounts of Jesus in order to prove Jesus' existence?
2. As one atheist has charged, do we need to have historical writings from during Jesus' lifetime to prove that Jesus existed? Why is it improbable that we will ever find non-Christian writings about Jesus from days in which he lived?
3. Why is it the case that any historian who rejected the existence of Jesus would also have to reject the existence of Tiberius Caesar?
4. Create a chart listing the five authors of the sources used above, the name of the source (the title of the book), when the source was written, and what facts we can discover about Jesus from each.

People to Remember

Tiberius Caesar Augustus
Tacitus
Josephus
Suetonius
Pliny the Younger
Jewish Talmud

Memory Verse Options

John 8:58
Galatians 2:20
Hebrews 13:8

Going Beyond the Call of Duty: Readings for the Overachiever

Geisler, Norman and Frank Turek. *I Don't Have Enough Faith to be an Atheist*. Wheaton: Crossway Books, 2004.

Habermas, Gary. *The Historical Jesus: Ancient Evidence for the Life of Christ*. Joplin: College Press, 1996.

Chapter 10

The Historicity of Christianity:
The Authority of the Bible

"I do indeed think that we can now know almost nothing concerning the life and personality of Jesus . . . "[1]

—Rudolph Bultmann

Biblical Critics

SINCE THE evidence is definitive that Jesus definitely existed, most who deny the historicity of Jesus do not do so on the grounds that he never existed, but rather that no one can know the personality and the character of Jesus Christ. In the nineteenth century, German scholars began searching for the "Historical Jesus" in hopes of stripping away the myth that surrounded him and finding the true person who was Jesus Christ. Rudolph Bultmann, a former leader of the Historical Jesus movement stated, "Of course the doubt as to whether Jesus really existed is unfounded and not worth refutation. No sane person can doubt that Jesus stands as founder behind the historical movement whose first distinct stage is represented by the Palestinian community."[2] While Bultmann and the others did not doubt Jesus existed, they did hold that Jesus is so immersed in mythology that no one can know truly who he was.

Today's version of this mythology campaign is the Jesus Seminar. In 1993 the Jesus Seminar published *The Five Gospels: The Search for the Authentic Words of Jesus.* This book contains over 1,500 sayings of Jesus in which the scholars of the Jesus Seminar decided whether or not Jesus actually said each statement. According to the Jesus Seminar website, "It was deemed entirely consonant with the mission of the Jesus Seminar to

---

[1] Rudolf Bultmann, *Jesus and the Word* (New York: Charles Scribner's Sons, 1934), 8.

[2] Ibid., 13.

decide whether, after careful review of the evidence, a particular saying or parable did or did not fairly represent the voice of the historical Jesus."[3] Therefore, if you come across a copy of this book in a library or bookstore, you will notice the words therein are color-coded. If the words are in red, then Jesus actually said those words. If in pink, Jesus likely said them. If gray, then it is likely that Jesus did not say the words. And if in black, then Jesus definitely did not utter those words. After investigation of the book, you will realize that they believe that only 2% of the gospels were definitely stated by Jesus, while 82% were definitely not said by Jesus at all![4]

It is not hard to recognize the fault of these scholars; they do not think that the Bible is historical or authentic. They believe that somehow and someway myth and falsehood have slipped into God's Word. Yet if the source of our information about Jesus is corrupt, then our concepts and ideas about Christianity have been corrupted as well.

The Historicity of the Bible

Since it has already been proven that Jesus existed, our next step is to prove that his sayings, actions, and personality are grounded in history. The source of all of this information is found in one book: the Bible. Therefore, if it can be proven that the Bible is accurate, authoritative, and trustworthy, then it has also been proven that the contents therein are historical. Of course, there are in-depth studies of specific events in the Bible, for instance the crucifixion and the resurrection; but there is not enough room to take on such endeavors here. In fact, it must be noted that most of the information in this chapter will focus on only half of the Bible: the New Testament. This is not due to some dismissal of the Old Testament, but rather because of the Christian's foremost need to prove the actions and personality of Jesus Christ.[5]

There are three approaches to our study on the historicity and inerrancy of God's Word: The bibliographical approach, the internal evidence, and the external evidence. While each of these areas deal with independent issues, it will be observed how each contributes a significant role in our proof for the historicity of the Bible.

---

[3] http://westarinstitute.org/.

[4] Geisler, *Baker Encyclopedia of Christian Apologetics*, 387.

[5] Further study in the area of Old Testament proof can be found in Josh McDowell's *The New Evidence that Demands a Verdict*.

The Bibliographical Approach

The Bibliographical approach brings to light the **manuscript** evidence for the Bible. A manuscript is merely a handwritten copy of the original work. Therefore, when taken in reference to Biblical matters, manuscripts can help us to demonstrate that the copies are actually very similar if not exactly the same as what the original inspired writers had written two thousand years ago. The apparent struggle in this method is that scholars do not have any original autographs from the inspired writers of the Bible. It is very likely that these original writings were ruined from being constantly transported and from general overuse. While it may seem that this would derail our mission, the lack of an original does not eliminate the prospect of finding what the original said.

Take for instance a love note. Let's imagine that, once upon a time, a teacher picked up a love note that was circulated around the class. The note was already torn, frayed, and was hardly readable. But the words in that love note struck a chord with that teacher; she saved the note and put it in her desk. However the words did not stay in her desk; she used them constantly. She would quote parts of the note in her holiday cards to her family, she printed a copy for all of her lady-friends, and even re-wrote the entire note and gave it to her husband. What if I then told you that the note was actually written one thousand years ago and the teacher lived in Medieval Europe? While the original of this letter would never be found, would it be possible to find out what it said? Actually, depending on the existence of manuscripts, it would be quite possible to determine what was written on the note. The first thing we would have to do is find every copy of the letter that was in existence. Whether the copies were in England, Africa, or China, they must be tracked down and investigated. Of course, the more copies of this manuscript that were found, the greater the likelihood we could decipher what the original autograph said. Also, generally speaking, the earlier the copy, the greater the likelihood that it represented what was in the original. And lastly, the similarities between these letters would give credible evidence of what was written in the original love note.

The same technique will be used to give evidence for the historicity of the Bible. The number of manuscripts, the time span between the writing of the book and of our earliest copies, and the consistency between the manuscripts will all be examined.

Number of Manuscripts—There is no doubt that the Bible has more manuscript copies than any other book from antiquity. Norman Geisler writes, "The New Testament text is preserved in some 5686 partial and complete manuscript portions that were copied by hand from the second (possibly even the first) through the fifteenth centuries."[6] If you examine the chart below, you will see that the Bible clearly prevails over all other books in antiquity. The closest document is Homer's *Iliad* which has a mere 643 copies! J. Harold Greenlee writes, "The number of available MSS [manuscripts] of the New Testament is overwhelmingly greater than those of any other work of ancient literature."[7] The fact of the matter is that scholars have more than enough manuscripts to determine what the original autograph said.

The Time Span—The next facet of our journey is to discover the time span between when the book was actually written and the oldest known manuscript that is still in existence. The further the manuscript is from its original writing, the more likely that it could have been accidentally corrupted by copyists.

By looking again at the chart below, you will discover that for most ancient historical documents the earliest manuscript is approximately dated 1,000 years after the original was written. The only manuscripts that are comparable to the New Testament are from Homer's *Iliad*. The earliest manuscripts for this work were written 400 years after the original. In comparison, there is a *complete* New Testament manuscript from within 250 years of its conception. J. Harold Greenlee again agrees: "The earliest extant MSS of the NT were written much closer to the date of the original writing than is the case in almost any other piece of ancient literature."[8]

---

[6] Norman Geisler, *Baker Encyclopedia of Christian Apologetics*, 532.

[7] Harold J. Greenlee, *Introduction to New Testament Textual Criticism,* (Grand Rapids: Eerdmans Publishing, 1977), 15.

[8] Ibid., 15.

The manuscript evidence chart:[9]

Author	Book	Date Written (Approx.)	Earliest Extant Manuscript Copy	Time Span (in years)	# of Manu-scripts
Homer	*Iliad*	800 B.C.	400 B.C.	400	643
Herodotus	*History*	450 B.C	A.D. 900	1,350	8
Plato	*Tetralogies*	400 B.C.	A.D. 900	1,300	7
Aristotle	*Ode to Poetics*	350 B.C.	A.D.1100	1,450	49
Demosthenes		300 B.C.	A.D.1100	1,400	200
Caesar	*Gallic War*	50 B.C.	A.D. 900	950	10
Livy	*Roman History*	30 B.C.	A.D. 300 (frag.) A.D. 900	330 930	1 19
Pliny the Elder	*Natural History*	A.D.80	A.D. 850	770	7
Josephus	*The Jewish War*	A.D. 90	A.D. 900	810	9
Tacitus	*Annals*	A.D.100	A.D. 850 A.D.1000	750 900	1 19
New Testament Authors	*New Testament*	A.D. 50-100	A.D. 125 (frag.) A.D.200 (books) A.D. 350 (complete N.T.)	50 100 250	5,686[1]

Consistent Manuscripts—The question remains, with all of these man-uscripts, how similar are they to each other? Before diving into consistency, the task of the textual critic should be analyzed. Let's hypothesize that A in the chart[10] below is the original book of Mark that was written around A.D. 50. The divergent lines represent different copies of the original,

[9] The content of this chart was taken from three major sources: McDowell's *New Evidence that Demands a Verdict*, Strobel's *The Case for Christ*, and an interview with John Ankerberg and Norman Geisler called, "The Bible: Can we Trust it?" See Readings for the Overachiever at the end of the chapter for more details.

[10] Chart developed from Sir Frederic Kenyon's *Our Bible and the Ancient Manuscripts*, 1895.

which results in copies of copies and so forth. Also, the dates have been added on the left, so that you can know when each theoretical manuscript was written. Therefore A is the original and was written in A.D. 50, B and C were copied in A.D.100, D–F in A.D. 150 and so forth. To make the illustration more accurate, it should be stated that each of the major divisions, say D, E, F, and G, have all traveled to different areas of the world. Therefore, the copies that follow these four manuscripts will likely be found in these same areas.

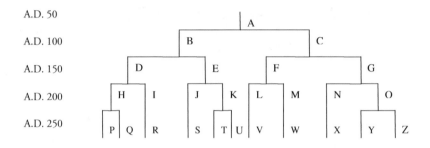

The first thing to point out is the actual role of consistency. Of course, the scholar is prepared to investigate how consistent all of these manuscripts are, but it is much more complicated than simply comparing them. Let's suggest that a **variant** is discovered in manuscript "D." A variant is simply an instance where the manuscript was copied incorrectly, even evidencing miniscule differences, and then that variant is unintentionally transmitted to every copy that follows. These variants are usually misspellings and occasionally an added word. Unfortunately, everything copied from "D" (and below it in the chart) will have this variant. Of course, variants are disconcerting, but the brighter side of this problem is that all of the other manuscripts not derived from "D" do not have this specific variant, so the textual critic is able to easily discover and correct the variant before it reaches today's Bible.

With this in mind, one must wonder if there are any variants that are not easily remedied. The late Wescott and Hort, two of America's champions of textual criticism determined, "The amount of what can in any sense be called substantial variation is but a small fraction of the whole . . . and can hardly form more than a thousandth part of the entire text." [11] This minor fraction of the Bible isn't in question because a part of the

---

[11] Brooker Foss Westcott and Fenton John Anthony Hort, *The New Testament in the Original Greek* (London: Macmillan, 1881), 2.

Bible is missing; but rather, no one is certain which manuscript has the right reading. For instance, in the chart above, if B and C both have a conflict, how could you determine which is correct? In these instances, one of the readings is put in the Bible, and if you have a good Bible, the variant will be listed in the footnotes. Geisler adds, "the problem is not that we don't *know what* the text is, but that we are not *certain which* text has the right reading. We have 100 percent of the New Testament and we are sure about 99.5 percent of it."[12] The fact of the matter is that the Bible has a very consistent set of manuscripts that have been adequately examined by competent Christian and secular scholars. These scholars have determined that, beyond a very small percentage, the Bible we hold in our hands is exactly what the original authors wrote.

The Internal Evidence

In this section two lines of arguments will be made. It will be demonstrated that the writers of the New Testament were eyewitnesses to the events in the New Testament and that the writers wrote their words down during the age of other eyewitnesses.

First, the importance of the first line of argumentation is straightforward: it is crucial to show that the writers were there when it happened, or at least, in the vein of Mark and Luke, that they interviewed people who were there when it happened. There is no doubt that the Bible itself claims that the disciples were eyewitnesses. Hank Hanegraaff, known to many as radio's "Bible Answer Man," reminds us of these claims, "Luke, who wrote the books of Luke and Acts, says that he gathered eyewitness testimony and 'carefully investigated everything' (Luke 1:1–3). Peter reminded his readers that the disciples 'were eyewitnesses of [Jesus'] majesty' and 'did not follow cleverly invented stories' (2 Pet. 1:16). Truly, the Bible affirms the *eyewitness* credibility of its writers."[13]

While the claims of the Bible are very important, you have to admit that to a non-Christian who does not believe in the Bible, the claims of the Bible may be less than convincing. Therefore these three D's have been formulated. The three D's stand for Details, Digits, and Deaths.

The first D, Details, is simply the recognition that the stories told by the eyewitnesses were very detailed accounts. These stories were so detailed

---

[12] Norman Geisler and Ron Brooks, *When Skeptics Ask* (Wheaton: Victor Books, 1990), 159.

[13] Hank Hanegraaff , "M-A-P-S to Guide You through Biblical Reliability" [Internet] http://www.equip.org/free/DB011.htm.

that they would only have been possible by eyewitness testimony. Also, those who claim that the gospels are myth neglect to take the details into account. Most other mythological literature is not written in the style of the gospels. The gospels were written as detailed eyewitness accounts, not myth.

The second D, Digits, signifies the number of men that it took to write the New Testament. Nine men, with God's help, wrote every book. The fact of the matter is that it would be impossible for nine men to independently write twenty-seven books that corroborated each other's detailed stories unless they were truly eyewitnesses of these events, or at least had interviewed eyewitnesses. If they were liars, their conspiracy would likely have ended with one of them spilling the beans. Also, if nine men were to start such a conspiracy, wouldn't they have made themselves out to be exemplary men of the faith? But the fact of the matter is that the authors wrote derogatory remarks about themselves. If the authors were liars, they simply would have omitted these remarks.

While the topic of the last D may seem a little morbid, the deaths of the disciples were very significant events. Ten of the original twelve disciples, save Judas who committed suicide and John who was exiled on the island of Patmos, were tortured and executed for their beliefs. Even the apostle Paul was martyred for his views. As you saw in Pliny's letter in the last chapter, it was probable that the Roman officials who questioned each disciple gave them a chance to recant their views. You may be wondering, "But haven't some people in history died for a lie?" This question may help: Were the men who flew planes into the twin towers on 9/11 rewarded by entrance into heaven? If not, then they died for what they thought was the truth, but was actually a falsehood. Now rethink this question, would these same men have flown into the towers if they *knew* that what they believed was a lie? The point here is simply that if the ten disciples and Paul the apostle *knew* that Jesus did not do what the Bible says he did, why wouldn't they have renounced their faith? They could have simply said, "I am not a Christian," cursed Christ and worshiped Caesar, and they probably would have gotten off with a few lashes. Instead, they died for what they had seen and heard. They knew it was the truth because they had seen it for themselves.

On to our second line of argumentation; it is important to show that these apostles wrote early. This is important for two reasons: if the New Testament was written after the 1st century, then it simply was too late to be authored by the apostles. This would damage the first line of argumentation: that eyewitnesses wrote the Bible. Along the same lines, if it were written later, then there would be time for myth and legend to develop and be added to the Biblical text. Yet since the New Testament was written during the time that eyewitnesses were still alive, the readers of the Gospels would have known if the apostles were telling the truth! Paul understands this situation and makes use of it, "He [Jesus] appeared to more than five hundred of the brothers at the same time, most of whom are still living, though some have fallen asleep."[14] In other words, Paul tells his readers "Hey if you don't believe me, there are many others that saw with their own eyes. You can ask them if you would like."

There is no doubt that the New Testament was written during the first century. One of the greatest evidences for this fact is that there are early letters written by church fathers that contain quotes from the Bible. For instance, Ignatius, Bishop of Antioch at the end of the first century, wrote seven epistles and included quotes from 15 of the New Testament books. The point here is that in order for Ignatius to be quoting these books, they must have existed before he quoted them! Therefore there is no doubt that these books were written during the first century. [15]

Next, attention is turned to the New Testament itself to prove its early writing. For instance, at the end of Acts in 28:30 it reads, "For two whole years Paul stayed there in his own rented house and welcomed all who came to see him." Now why this is interesting because Paul was in Rome, a place where Nero eventually captured, tortured, and killed Christians. In the Acts passage, Paul is not being persecuted and has not yet been martyred. Therefore we can assume that when Luke completed Acts the persecution had not yet begun. Since the persecution began around A.D. 62, you can assume that Acts was written during or prior to this year. Since Luke was written before Acts, it must have been written prior to 62. Therefore, conservative scholars are confident that Luke was written between A.D. 55–60. Lastly, note that the destruction of the temple in Jerusalem took place in A.D. 70; this event is not recorded in any of the New Testament![16] Since it seems that an event of such epic proportions would have been included if it happened during the time of the writing, most conservative scholars argue that none of the New Testament was written beyond A.D. 70, except for perhaps John and Revelation.

The most impressive piece of early authorship that is known to exist is a piece of manuscript evidence. The John Ryland's fragment is currently

[14] 1 Cor. 15:6.

[15] See section on external evidence for more citations of church fathers.

[16] Some argue that this event is implied in Revelation.

housed in the John Ryland's library in Manchester, England. Conservative scholars date the fragment from around A.D. 125. Until this fragment of the book of John was found, most liberal scholars assumed that the fourth gospel was actually written after A.D. 150. For those who miss the implication, a dating this late would indicate that the apostle John did not write the work. This fragment of the book of John changed all of that. Since this fragment was found a substantial distance from where the author wrote, more time is needed to account for copying and carrying the manuscript to Egypt. Therefore, since this fragment is dated at the first quarter of the second century and was found in distant Egypt, it is very likely that the apostle John wrote his work around A.D. 70–80. The John Ryland's Library website reads, "[the fragment] ranks as the earliest known fragment of the New Testament in any language. It provides us with invaluable evidence of the spread of Christianity in areas distant from the land of its origin; it is particularly interesting to know that among the books read by the early Christians in Upper Egypt was St. John's Gospel, commonly regarded as one of the latest of the books of the New Testament."[17]

While more specifics could be mentioned, the point has been made. If most or all of the New Testament was written during the first century, the authors were likely eyewitnesses and the books were written fairly early in comparison to the time in which the events actually happened. For instance, Luke was likely written between A.D. 55–60, and around thirty years after the crucifixion of Jesus. How does this compare with other religious literature? Lee Strobel, in his *Case for Christ*, writes:

> Although the Galas of Zoraster, about 1000 B.C., are believed to be authentic, most of the Zorastrian scriptures were not put into writing until after the third century A.D. The most popular Parsi biography of Zoraster was written in A.D. 1278. The scriptures of Buddha, who lived in sixth century B.C., were not put into writing until after the Christian era . . . Although we have the sayings of Muhammad, who lived from A.D. 570 to 632, in the Koran, his biography was not written until 767—more than a full century after his death. So the situation of Jesus is unique-and quite impressive . . .[18]

Compared to other religious scripture, the Bible was written very close to the events it describes. Therefore, Strobel's implication that the

[17] The John Ryland's Library of Manchester website for the fragment is: http://rylibweb.man.ac.uk/data1/dg/text/fragment.htm.
[18] Lee Strobel, *Case for Christ* (Grand Rapids: Zondervan, 1998), 86–87.

Bible is a unique document is very true. Christians have a book of historical accounts by eyewitnesses that wrote very near to the time of the actual events.

The External Evidence

Another convincing proof that the Bible is historical is evidence found in sources that are outside the Bible. The last chapter dealt with a wealth of external evidence: the writings of first and second century non-Christians. The non-Christian sources not only informed you that Jesus existed, but they also told a little about his followers and the Romans' dealings with the early church. The fact of the matter is that these writings support the historical account found in scripture. Now two more sources of external evidence will be examined: the early church fathers and the findings in archaeology.

Using the writings from early church fathers from the first four centuries, apologists are able to demonstrate the accuracy of the New Testament. Earlier we went through all of the manuscript evidence and found these copies are numerous, early, and consistent. But let's put this evidence aside and show how the early church fathers support the claim that the Bible is accurate to the originals. Norman Geisler explains:

> "If you destroyed every Bible in the world, all of those almost 6,000 manuscripts, all of the translations in Latin and Ethiopic and Coptic and every other language, if you destroyed every Bible in the world, we could still reconstruct virtually the whole Bible from quotations from the early Fathers. One scholar studied the Ante-Nicene Fathers and he concluded there were 36,289 quotes from the New Testament in these early Fathers. That means every verse in the New Testament except eleven, most of which come from 3 John, are found in these Fathers. You could destroy every Bible in the world and still reconstruct virtually the whole New Testament just from these quotations of the Fathers."[19]

While the manuscripts are invaluable to our proof of Biblical accuracy, the early church fathers made wide use of the New Testament; so much so that almost the entire Bible can be derived from their writings! This demonstrates that the Bible is consistent and that Christians have an accurate copy of what the original authors wrote.

---

[19] John Ankerberg and Norman Geisler, "The Bible: Can we Trust it?" [Internet] http://www.ankerberg.org/Articles/_PDFArchives/islam/2Geisler(3)-The Bible Can We Trust It.pdf.

Secondly, it should be understood that there has never been an archaeological find that contradicts God's Word. Nelson Glueck, a famous Jewish archaeologist wrote, "It may be stated categorically that no archaeological discovery has ever controverted a biblical passage. Scores of archaeological findings have been made which confirm in clear outline or exact detail historical statements in the Bible."[20] There are many, many archaeological finds that could be listed here. For instance, archaeologists have the **ossuary**, or the bone box, of high priest Joseph Caiaphas.[21] They also have found a stone slab that reads, "Pontius Pilate, Prefect of Judea."

Not to neglect the Old Testament, there have been just as many, or more findings, to authenticate the earlier books of the Bible. A tablet from 900 B.C. was found inscribed with "House of David." And probably the most important archaeological discovery to date: the Dead Sea Scrolls. The scrolls, found in 1947 at Qumran, included a manuscript of the entire book of Isaiah written around 100 B.C. Until this time, the oldest complete copy of Isaiah was from the 9th century A.D.! The most interesting thing about the copy found at Qumran was that the writing was exactly the same as the copy written one thousand years later! The scroll showed that the copyists of the Old Testament accurately hand-copied this book for over a thousand years! Again, there is no doubt that archaeological finds have managed to strengthen our argument for the Bible.

The Importance of Biblical Inerrancy

Peter denied that any myth had slipped into the authors' accounts, "We did not follow cleverly invented stories when we told you about the power and coming of our Lord Jesus Christ, but we were eyewitnesses of his majesty."[22] Peter understood the importance and truth of Biblical Inerrancy. The term **inerrancy** simply means that God's Word is without error. Where most people are confused on this issue is how inerrancy applies to the Bible that you hold in your hands today. The term inerrancy only explicitly applies to the original **autographs** of the Bible. In other words, what God inspired and the men wrote onto their parchment was completely without error.

There is no doubt that inerrancy is Biblically supported. Jesus acknowledged this doctrine when he declared, "the Scripture cannot be bro-

[20] Nelson Glueck, "Rivers in the Desert" (Philadelphia: Jewish Publication Society, 1969), 31.
[21] Matt. 26:3.
[22] 1 Pet. 2:16.

ken."[23] There is also a philosophical tactic to prove inerrancy: If God is perfect then God's Word must be perfect. God is perfect. Therefore God's Word must be perfect. So, if the claim that the original autographs contained errors is correct, then God must not have authored the books of the Bible. Rejecting this doctrine affects your view of the nature of God and allows for the possibility that God is not the mastermind behind the Bible. For if God wrote an imperfect book, then he must be imperfect, and an imperfect being is not God at all! On the other hand, if God did not write the Bible, then why are Christians following it? Can you trust it? Without inerrancy, you reject the infinite and perfect nature of God and lose trust and confidence in God's message.

A man of integrity and honesty cannot state that there aren't difficulties in today's Bible. Merely due to the continuous copying and translation after translation of God's Word, humanity is likely to make mistakes. Christians agree that God inspired the authors of the Bible, while the copyist and translators were never given inspirational status. Do not be dismayed, the Bible you have on your desk is still "God-breathed and is useful for teaching, rebuking, correcting and training in righteousness,"[24] but Christians need to take an honest look at some of the proposed problems that lie within.

Already you may see a noticeable contradiction in logic: The Bible is God's infallible Word, yet it contains apparent problems. At face value it seems that this is a contradiction, but actually it is not. First, the "problems" that appear in the Bible are usually easily explained by competent scholars and often turn out not to be errors at all!

These problems usually are a result of faulty interpretation or simply a misunderstanding of 1st century culture and language. The parts that could rightly be called "problematic" are due to the men who were copying the Bible. While the scribes were very meticulous and the errors are very rare, a letter or number could have been missed or accidentally added. Usually this would be noticed when the copied page was reread, especially if the problem was with a letter. Yet there are instances where numbers are problematic. Two proponents of inerrancy, Norman Geisler and Thomas Howe, explain in their *When Critics Ask: A Popular Handbook on Bible Difficulties*, "While present copies of Scripture are very good, they are not without error. For example, 2 Kings 8:26 gives the age of King Ahaziah as twenty-two, whereas 2 Chronicles 22:2 says forty-two. The later number

---

[23] John 10:35.

[24] 2 Tim. 3:16.

cannot be correct, or he would have been older than his father. This is obviously a copyist error, but it does not alter the inerrancy of the original."[25] Notice that the contradiction here did not leave the authors with a major dilemma, they simply realized which of the two accounts was accurate, then moved on. Many of the Bible's problematic areas can easily be dealt with, and the reader can discover the inerrant words that were originally written by the inspired author of the work.

If a skeptic throws an apparent Biblical "error" in your face, be calm and confident that there is an adequate explanation to the problem. Write down the issue and the verses and be prepared to do a little research. Let the skeptic know that you would like to discuss it with him later and move on to other topics. Likely you will need to find a book on problematic passages in the Bible such as the ones offered in the "readings for overachievers" section at the end of the chapter. Take your time to investigate, then return to the skeptic to answer his objection. Honestly, skeptics of this type may simply be out to frustrate you and you may find yourself constantly doing research to answer their questions. Let the Holy Spirit guide you to determine if you should continue to minister to this individual. It may get to the point where you simply buy a book for him and let him do his own research!

Summary

There is no doubt that the authenticity and inerrancy of God's Word is under severe attack. If no one is willing to defend God's Word, this may result in the Bible being treated as merely a mythical story with no insight or authority in our daily lives. By looking at manuscript evidence, internal evidence, and external evidence, it has been demonstrated that the Bible is an accurate depiction of historical events. Students should not be afraid to put their trust in the Word of God. Its historical accuracy has been verified by Christian and non-Christian sources as well as the archaeological community at large.

Study Questions

1. Explain the three different types of evidence used to prove that the Bible is historically accurate (Bibliographical, Internal, External).

---

[25] Norman Geisler and Thomas Howe, *When Critics Ask : A Popular Handbook on Bible Difficulties* (Wheaton: Victor Books, 1992), 23.

2. Which of these three lines of argument do you find most compelling? Why? (Remember that the previous chapter falls in the category of "External Evidence.")

3. Why is it important to show that we have many manuscripts of the New Testament?

4. How would you argue against a person that states that the Gospels, especially the book of John, were written after A.D. 150?

5. What is the difference between the "time span" discussed in the Bibliographical section and the "apostles wrote early" in the internal evidence section?

Terms to Consider

Inerrancy

Autographs

Manuscript

Variant

Ossuary

Memory Verse Options

2 Tim. 3:16

Going Beyond the Call of Duty: Readings for the Overachiever

Ankerberg, John and Norman Geisler. "The Bible: Can we Trust it?" [Internet] http://www.ankerberg.org/Articles/_PDFArchives/islam/2Geisler(3)-The Bible Can We Trust It.pdf.

Archer, Gleason. *New International Encyclopedia of Bible Difficulties.* Grand Rapids: Zondervan, 2001.

Geisler, Norman and Thomas Howe. *When Critics Ask: A Popular Handbook on Bible Difficulties.* Wheaton: Victor Books, 1992.

Kaiser, Walter C., Peter H. Davids, F. F. Bruce, and Manfred T. Brauch. *Hard Sayings of the Bible.* Downers Grove: Intervarsity Press, 1996.

McDowell, Josh. *The New Evidence that Demands a Verdict.* Nashville: Thomas Nelson, 1999.

Strobel, Lee. *The Case for Christ.* Grand Rapids: Zondervan, 1998.

Chapter 11

The Historicity of Christianity:
The Trinity and the Deity of Jesus

"The Father is God, and the Son God, and the Holy Spirit God,
and yet that this Trinity is not three Gods, but one God."[1]
—St. Augustine

A Shocking Revelation

SOME CHRISTIANS treat the concept of the Trinity like a stain on the living room floor. They attempt to cover it up like it is something to hide because it's much too perplexing to explain. This sort of negative attitude toward our most foundational creed needs serious adjustment! Christians must remember that the Trinity, and specifically Christ's deity, was the revelation that sparked the flame of our religion. C. S. Lewis explains the phenomena in his *Mere Christianity*:

> Then comes the real shock. Among these Jews there suddenly turns up a man who goes about talking as if He was God. He claims to forgive sins. He says He has always existed. He says He is coming to judge the world at the end of time. Now let us get this clear. Among Pantheists, like the Indians, anyone might say that he was a part of God, or one with God: there would be nothing very odd about. But this man, since He was a Jew, could not mean that kind of God. God, in their language, meant the Being outside the world who had made it and was infinitely different from anything else. And when you have grasped that, you will see that what this man said was, quite simply, the most shocking thing that has ever been uttered by human lips.[2]

[1] Augustine, *De Trinitate (On the Trinity)*, I. 5.8.
[2] C. S. Lewis, *Mere Christianity*, 55.

While explaining how Jesus, the Holy Spirit, and the Father are all one God may take some explaining and may not result in 100% proof, we as Christians must be willing to attempt to accurately explain our concept of God to the best of our abilities.

A "Mystery" of the Faith

The first issue we must conquer concerning the Holy Trinity is simply the concept that the Trinity is not objectively provable apart from the Word of God. Unlike our evidence for God's existence, we have no evidence concerning the existence of three persons in God, barring the evidence found in Scripture. This does not limit the possibility that God, in reality, exists in three persons; but rather, simply shows that we need to understand the limitations of the evidence that can be used in defense of our belief.

To illustrate this point, consider a random and unknown student that you have seen on campus. What can you know about this person without doing some "research?" Simply speaking, without investigation, you could only know the things that are true of every human. You could know that they eat, sleep, need water and food to live, were born and will one day die, among many other facts. But until this person *reveals* things to you, you will not know that they like pizza, enjoy kung-fu movies, and deeply love their pet hamster. While it is agreed that the Trinity is a much deeper issue than simply an opinion about food, it is still something that cannot be known unless God reveals it. Thus, God's own revelation through Scripture can be our only source of evidence.

Secondly, while it can be shown that the concept of the Trinity is free from contradiction, it cannot be demonstrated exactly how one being can consist of three persons. We do not have a common day example of such a thing or even a "perfect analogy" to use as demonstration. We must come to the realization that humans will never be able to fully comprehend the infinite being, even when we get to heaven. Does this inability to fully comprehend the Trinity disprove its possibility? No! This limitation of our ability to understand the innermost details of the most complex being does, in no way, lead a person to believe that this being does not exist. It again merely shows our limitations to completely comprehend the perfect and infinite being.

Our task as Christian apologists is to adequately explain the correct view of the Trinity, to show that the doctrine is without logical contradiction, and to have some Biblical references to support our view.

Is the Trinity Logical?

One of the most widely argued critiques of the Trinity is that the concept is "illogical." Arguments against the Trinity usually entail a confusion and misrepresentation of what we actually believe about the Trinity; and therefore, a strawman fallacy is frequently committed. For instance, most Muslims would argue that it is ridiculous to believe that three Gods are actually one. Of course, we do not believe there are three Gods, but one God who is three in person. If we did believe that three completely separate Gods are actually one God, then we would have a serious contradiction on our hands, and *only then* would the concept of the Trinity be illogical.

The confusion and lack of understanding doesn't simply fall on the side of people who have a different faith than our own. Even Christians get confused when discussing the Trinity. Therefore, before going into detail on the orthodox view of the Trinity, some heretical views will be examined so that you will be able to recognize these erroneous ideas.

What the Trinity is Not

Tritheism—There are two major heresies that Christians should avoid when discussing the Trinity. The first heresy is Tritheism. This is simply the concept that Jesus, the Father, and the Holy Spirit are completely separate from each other. In other words, Tritheism means three separate Gods. If Tritheism were correct, there would be three completely separate persons, three separate beings, which would each be called "God." Essentially, if Christians held to Tritheism, we would be polytheists, just like the Hindus and the theistic Buddhists.

Tritheism Three Gods		
Deity (Nature)	Deity (Nature)	Deity (Nature)
△	◯	▢
Father (Person)	Jesus Christ (Person)	Holy Spirit (Person)

Not only is this view philosophically ridiculous,[3] but it is also Biblically inaccurate. Deuteronomy 6:4 reads, "Hear, O Israel: The Lord our God, the Lord is *one*." While some may wonder if this is a remark relegated to only the Old Testament community, note that Jesus himself quoted Deuteronomy 6:4 in Mark 12:29 when discussing the greatest commandment. Paul also reinforced the idea in 1 Corinthians 8:6. There is no doubt that the unity of God is founded on God's Word.

Modalism—The most common misunderstanding of the Trinity is called modalism. Oftentimes, Christians attempt to use the "ice/water/ water vapor" analogy to describe the Trinity. Unfortunately, this is a prime example of Modalism and is quite heretical. Modalism is simply the concept that God is one person, yet appears in three forms: Father, Son, and Holy Spirit. This would be sort of like an actor playing three different parts in a play. He appears on stage as three different personas, yet in reality, he is only one being.

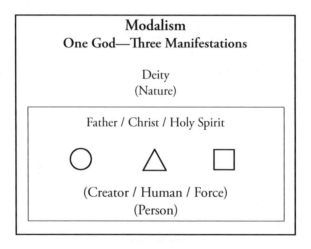

If modalism were true, it would be possible to diagnose our God with a multiple personality disorder. If you look at scripture, these three "forms" of God communicate and fellowship with each other. Yet if these three forms are actually the same being, why and how could this being communicate with itself? For instance, in the Garden of Gethsemane Jesus prayed, "I have brought you glory on earth by completing your work you gave me to do"[4] and "Righteous Father, although the world does not know

---

[3] See chapter 6, under the critique of polytheism.
[4] John 17:4.

you, I know you, and they know that you have sent me."[5] There are many other similar instances such as these where it seems, if modalism is correct, that God was talking to himself!

In reality, it seems as though when Jesus was in prayer, he was talking to another person: his Father in heaven. In addition, we have a Biblical account of all three "manifestations" of God showing up at the same time! In Mark 1:9–11, Jesus is being baptized as the Father speaks and the Holy Spirit descends on Jesus. Yet if these are all the same being, how is He taking three different forms at the same time? In conclusion, if modalism is correct, and each of the divine persons are simply modes of one being's existence, Christians would be left with a mentally deficient and confused being who would most likely be labeled as an acute schizophrenic.

Arianism and the Topic of the Incarnation

Some argue that believers created the Doctrine of the Trinity at the councils of Nicea and Constantinople[6] in the fourth century. These arguments are a result of the lack of knowledge of the writings of the early church fathers and a basic understanding of why these councils were called together. There is no doubt that the Trinity was widely agreed upon by the early church fathers, yet in the fourth century, a priest openly disagreed with the doctrine. Therefore, the council of Nicea was called to investigate and eventually denounce Arianism and to set the official doctrine "in stone" so that there could be no further disagreements about the orthodox position of the church. Dr. Geisler explains, "At the Ecumenical Council of Nicea (A.D. 325) the church addressed the nature of the relationship between the Father and the Son with the resulting condemnation of Arianism. An Alexandrian priest named Arius (d. A.D. 250) held that, since God the Father was immutable and unique, the Son had to be a created being. Thus Arius rejected the orthodox view that Jesus was of the "same substance" as the Father. Under the influence of Athanasius, the Council made it clear that Jesus was of the same, not just similar, substance as the Father: 'begotten not made.'"[7]

Arius' claims against the Trinity were actually not of a Biblical nature, but were rather philosophical and, while misguided, were rather insight-

---

[5] John 17:25.

[6] In 381, the council of Constantinople reaffirmed the conclusions made at the council of Nicea, as well as clarified the divinity of the Holy Spirit.

[7] Norman Geisler and R.E. MacKenzie, *Roman Catholics and Evangelicals: Agreements and differences,* (Grand Rapids: Baker Books, 1995), 71.

ful. He simply believed that God, being unable to change, could not have "become human" in any sense of the word. He contended that the orthodox view of the incarnation would have caused an essential change in the nature of God. Yet, as seen in the section on finite godism, if God changes, then he must be finite and thus is not God at all! Therefore Arius believed that Jesus was not God at all, but was merely an extraordinary human that followed God's will.

On the contrary, Christians believe that Jesus had two natures, divine and human, that did not blend. This is why you hear so many teachers and preachers say that Jesus was fully God and fully man. He was of the divine nature, but also had the essential attributes and qualities of a human. Consider the following illustration:

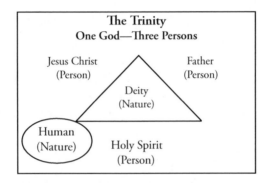

The triangle, while not a perfect analogy of the Trinity, shows how human nature was added to the divine while not "infecting" or in any way changing the infinite perfection of God. If Jesus' human nature is not actually a part of the divine nature, then no change in the divine nature has taken place. With this in mind, Arius' critique of the incarnation was dismantled. While Arianism was quickly deemed heretical, the incident did have a good result. The heretical priest's views forced the church to begin clarifying the doctrine, initially resulting in the Nicene Creed:

> We believe in ONE GOD THE FATHER Almighty, Maker of heaven and earth, and of all things visible and invisible. And in one LORD JESUS CHRIST, the only-begotten son of God, Begotten of the Father before all worlds, Light of Light, very God of very God, begotten, not made, Being of one substance with the Father; by whom all things were made . . . and in the HOLY GHOST, the Lord and Giver of Life; who proceeds from the Father; who with

the Father and the Son together is worshiped and glorified; who spake by the Prophets.[8]

Unity and Plurality: An Explanation of the Trinity

It is occasionally mentioned by liberal theologians that we should remove the word "Trinity" from the vocabulary of the Christian belief system. Some even mention that since the word is not found in Scripture, then it should not be used in Christian dogma. It should be pointed out that there are many words that we use to describe theological ideas that are not in the Bible; for instance, incarnation, rapture, and monotheism are not found in any accurate translation of the Word of God. But we cannot deduce that since these specific words are not in the Bible then the concepts that these words are representing aren't there either!

On the contrary, the Word of God does speak of a unity and plurality in the essence of God. Therefore, the Trinity is merely a word we use to speak of this complexity. Thomas Aquinas writes, "The name 'Trinity' in God signifies the determinate number of persons. And so the plurality of persons in God requires that we should use the word trinity."[9] Norman Geisler further explains, "[The Trinity] means that God is a triunity: He is a plurality within a unity. God has a plurality of persons and a unity of essence; God is three persons in one nature."[10]

To drive this point home, Scripture should be examined regarding the unity and plurality of God. As mentioned earlier in this chapter, there is no doubt that the Old and New Testament Jews believed that God was a unity. Deuteronomy 6:4, Mark 12:29, and 1 Corinthians 8:6 each explain the unity and simplicity of God. There is no doubt that the Bible describes God as ONE being.

In a little more complex fashion, the plurality of God should be discovered in the Word of God. This investigation will not result in an explicit citation in God's Word that states that "God is a Trinity; Jesus, the Father, and the Spirit are all God!" If you go looking for this sort of verification in the Bible, you will not find it. The closest you will find to an explicit description of the Trinity is found in Matthew 28:19, where Jesus

---

[8] Norman Geisler, *Baker Encyclopedia of Christian Apologetics,* 55.

[9] Aquinas, *Summa Theologica,* I.31.1.

[10] Norman Geisler, *Systematic Theology,* vol. 2, *God and Creation* (Minneapolis: Bethany House, 2003), 279.

commands, " . . . go and make disciples of all nations, baptizing them in the name of the Father, and of the Son and of the Spirit." This command is ripe with theological implications. Jesus is claiming that all three of these persons, himself included, are under the same "name." Note that "name" in the Old Testament denoted the nature of a being; that is why the ancient Jews found the names of God to be of so much importance. It also should be noted that Jesus' statement is a personal claim to divinity. Jesus is putting himself on the same divine plane as the Father. To Jews, this comment would have been blasphemous; if heard by the Sanhedrin, they likely would have tried to stone him to death on the spot.

Nevertheless, our search for explicit declarations of the Trinity will stop there in order to find the more prevalent implicit expressions of the plurality of God. While this may sound like it may be even more complicated than the last endeavor, take note that this is a relatively simple investigation. The task consists of observing the places in Scripture where God the Father, Jesus, and the Holy Spirit are shown to be divine. In other words, if the Bible makes these three out to be divine, and they are not the same person as expressed in modalism, then God must be a trinity!

Most people, Christians and non-Christians alike, have no qualms about whether or not we believe that the Father is God. Most of the Old Testament documents this belief, and this concept boils over into the New Testament. Usually when a writer mentions this idea, it is stated matter-of-factly, as if the readers should already fully comprehend that the Father is God. As a small sample of New Testament excerpts, take Philippians 2:11, ". . . every tongue should confess that Jesus Christ is Lord, to the glory of God the Father."[11]

While the Father's divinity is not questioned, some who have read the Bible disagree with our contention that Jesus is divine. In fact, many Christian cults do not believe that Jesus is a part of the divine nature. There are two ways to look at Christ's claims in connection with his divinity. First, there are specific times when Jesus claimed to be divine; and secondly, there are times where he claimed to have divine characteristics. To illustrate this distinction, notice the difference between, "I am God," and "I am omnipotent." The first is a specific claim to divinity, while the second is a claim to be able to do only what God could possibly perform.

While many treat Jesus as if he were merely a good man and not God, an inductive study of scripture reveals otherwise. One of the most obvious claims to divinity is rooted in an Old Testament story. When Moses met

---

[11] Philippians 2:11, (KJV).

God at the burning bush, the Father said to him, "I am who I am. This is what you are to say to the Israelites: 'I AM has sent me to you.'"[12] Turning to a discussion Jesus had with the Pharisees, Jesus makes this extraordinary claim: "'Your father Abraham rejoiced at the thought of seeing my day; he saw it and was glad.' 'You are not yet fifty years old,' the Jews said to him, 'and you have seen Abraham!' 'I tell you the truth,' Jesus answered, 'before Abraham was born, **I am!**' At this, they picked up stones to stone him, but Jesus hid himself, slipping away from the temple grounds."[13] In this instance the Jews, knowing their Hebrew Scriptures, knew exactly what Jesus was implying. He was claiming to be eternal, a quality only God has, and to be the one and only "I am." They became so angry that they picked up stones and Jesus had to escape from feeling their wrath![14]

There is also ample evidence to show that Jesus claimed to be the Messiah and the Son of God. Luke said that Jesus explained to the disciples how the Old Testament proclaimed his coming, "And beginning with Moses and all the Prophets, he [Jesus] explained to them what was said in all the Scriptures concerning himself."[15]

In a more specific instance, take this encounter with the Jewish high priest: "Again the high priest asked him, 'Are you the Christ, the Son of the Blessed One?'

'I am,' said Jesus. 'And you will see the Son of Man sitting at the right hand of the Mighty One and coming on the clouds of heaven.' The high priest tore his clothes.

'Why do we need any more witnesses?' he asked. 'You have heard the blasphemy. What do you think?' They all condemned him as worthy of death. Then some began to spit at him; they blindfolded him, struck him with their fists, and said, 'Prophesy!' And the guards took him and beat him."[16] Again Jesus' claims provoked the Pharisees to anger. They knew what he was saying, yet today many people miss the fact that Jesus and his disciples did believe that he was the Son of God, the Messiah, and part of the divine nature.

As a more tertiary investigation, here is a list of characteristics that are divine in nature and that were attributed to Jesus. As mentioned earlier, in John 8:58 and additionally John 17:5, Jesus claimed to have existed

---

[12] Exod. 3:14.

[13] John 8:56–59.

[14] As for other verses, John 20:28 includes Thomas' claim that Jesus is God and in Titus 2:13 Jesus is described as part of the divine nature.

[15] Luke 24:27.

[16] Mark 14: 61–64.

from eternity. In Mark 2:5 and Acts 5:31, Jesus is attributed the ability to forgive sins, an ability that only God has.

The Old Testament clarifies that it is God who brings and ends life, "The LORD brings death and makes alive,"[17] yet Jesus has this ability as well, "For just as the Father raises the dead and gives them life, even so the Son gives life to whom he is pleased to give it."[18]

One of the most convincing arguments is that Jesus accepted worship. While this may not initially seem overwhelming, realize that even angels are forbidden to accept worship.[19] Therefore when Jesus accepted worship in John 9:38, he admitted that he was no mere person or angel; he is God!

Additionally, Jesus claimed that he had been given all authority over the world[20], would judge the world[21], and asked his disciples to pray in his name.[22] Lastly, Paul's statement in the first chapter of Colossians will complete this section. Paul writes in Colossians 1:15–17, "He is the image of the invisible God . . . by him all things were created: things in heaven and on earth, visible and invisible, whether thrones or powers or rulers or authorities; all things were created by him and for him. He is before all things, and in him all things hold together." Paul contends that Jesus is God incarnate, that he created everything, has authority over everyone, and he sustains the existence of the world. It seems as though Paul understood the implications of Jesus' divinity.

Lastly, and no less importantly, the evidences for the deity of the Holy Spirit should be examined. It will be shown that the New Testament authors also undoubtedly believed that the Holy Spirit is God. Paul writes in 2 Corinthians 3:17, "Now the Lord is the Spirit, and where the Spirit of the Lord is, there is freedom."

Luke, reporting the words of Peter, states, "Then Peter said, 'Ananias, how is it that Satan has so filled your heart that you have lied to the Holy Spirit and have kept for yourself some of the money you received for the land? Didn't it belong to you before it was sold? And after it was sold, wasn't the money at your disposal? What made you think of doing such a

---

[17] 1 Sam. 2:6.

[18] John 5:21.

[19] see Rev. 22:8–9.

[20] Matthew 28:18–19.

[21] 2 Timothy 4:1.

[22] John 14:13–14.

thing? You have not lied to men but to God."[23] Peter's implication is clear. Ananias did not lie merely to man, but to the Holy Spirit who is God. This is why Ananias' act was such a mortal sin and had such a swift and severe punishment.

The Holy Spirit also possesses attributes of the divine being. For instance, the Psalmist claims to be unable to escape from the presence of the Holy Spirit. Thus Psalms 139:7–12 implies the Holy Spirit's omnipresence. In Hebrews 9:14, the author describes the Spirit as "eternal." Paul mentions in 1 Corinthians 2:10, "In the same way no one knows the thoughts of God except the Spirit of God." Yet if the Holy Spirit knows the innermost thoughts of God, then isn't he omniscient? Of course, the deeper implication quickly arises, if the Spirit knows the innermost thoughts of God, then he must be God!

Lastly, Norman Geisler adds, "[The Holy Spirit] is associated with God the Father in creation (Gen. 1:2). He is involved with other members of the Godhead in the work of redemption (John 3:5–6; Rom. 8:9–17, 26–27; Titus 3:5–7). He is associated with other members of the Trinity under the "name" of God (Matt. 28:18–20). Finally, the Holy Spirit appears, along with the Father and Son, in New Testament benedictions (for example, 2 Cor. 13:14)."[24]

Summary

Saint Augustine writes, "Some persons, however, find a difficulty in this faith; when they hear that the Father is God, and the Son God, and the Holy Spirit God, and yet that this Trinity is not three Gods, but one God."[25] There is no doubt that the Trinity and the deity of Christ are two of the most difficult doctrines of the church to explain and hopefully you have come to understand some of the complexities of our God; yet as you probably have realized, we cannot fully comprehend the innermost intricacies of the divine being. Therefore, beyond the Word of God, there is not much in the way of "proof" of God's triunity. Usually the Trinity and the deity of Christ is where run of the mill Theists and orthodox Christians part company. Christians, in trusting the inspired Word of God, must believe what it says, otherwise we would be mere theists who believe in God, but not his Son or Spirit.

---

[23] Acts 5:3–4.

[24] Geisler, *Baker Encyclopedia of Christian Apologetics,* 731.

[25] Augustine, *De Trinitate (On the Trinity),* I.5.8.

Study Questions

1. Explain why Jesus' revelation that he was God was so shocking to the Jewish community? If he was born into a pantheistic community, would the claim have been so shocking? Why or why not?
2. Describe the difference between Tritheism, and Modalism.
3. What did Arius believe about Jesus and how is it different from what we believe?
4. How did Arius' heretical views produce a beneficial consequence for the church?
5. In your *own words*, explain the Trinity.

Terms to Consider

Trinity
Modalism
Tritheism
Council of Nicea
Nicene Creed
Arianism

Memory Verse Options

Matthew 28:19

Going Beyond the Call of Duty: Readings for the Overachiever

Geisler, Norman. *Systematic Theology.* Vol. 2, *God and Creation.* Minneapolis: Bethany House, 2003.

(All graphics courtesy of Doug Beaumont at www.dougbeaumont.org.)

Chapter 12

The Moral Law:
An Introduction to Ethics

"How had I got this idea of just and unjust? A man does not call a line crooked unless he has some idea of a straight line. What was I comparing this universe with when I called it unjust?"[1]
—C. S. Lewis

Introduction

ONE OF the most interesting discussions that I ever heard was between two staff members at a Youth for Christ leadership meeting. For some reason, the discussion turned to ethics and this moral question: Was Rahab wrong for lying to the king's men? If you don't remember the story of Rahab, take a minute to look over the second chapter of Joshua. Two men had been sent into Jericho to spy out the land and bring a report back to Joshua and his militia. The king of Jericho found out about this plan and sent out men to find the Israelite spies. The spies had found solace at the house of a woman named Rahab, who happened to be a prostitute. When the king's men came to the door, she hid the Jews and lied to the soldiers. Since Rahab helped these men by lying, "Joshua spared Rahab the prostitute, with her family and all who belonged to her, because she hid the men Joshua had sent as spies to Jericho—and she lives among the Israelites to this day."[2] But this wasn't Rahab's only blessing from this act, she was listed as a woman of faith in Hebrews 11:31, was called "righteous" by James,[3] and was one of only three women mentioned in the lineage of Jesus![4] Yes, Rahab, a prostitute and gentile, was an ancestor of

[1] C. S. Lewis, *Mere Christianity*, 45.
[2] Josh. 6:25.
[3] Js. 2:25.
[4] Matt. 1:5.

the Son of God. The point being that God did not punish Rahab for this lie; it seemed that he blessed her for it!

The two people in the discussion did not come to any conclusions; in fact, it seemed as though they left at a stalemate. One held her ground that "If the Ten Commandments says it, then it is an absolute law that should never be broken." Her opponent argued that this could not be true and even offered this analogy, "Suppose you lived in Nazi Germany and you were hiding Jews in your home. If guards came to your door and asked, 'Do you have Jews in there?' would you tell them?" His answer was an emphatic "NO!"

This question cuts to the heart of ethics. **Ethics** is simply the field of study that deals with discovering what is morally right and wrong. In this chapter we will discuss the different theories of how men of different worldviews determine what is right behavior. First, we will investigate the claims of the naturalists, and then we will move on to the different theistic views of ethics.

The Naturalistic View of Ethics

The first realization that needs to occur is that every atheistic view of ethics rejects the possibility of having an absolute standard by which to judge what is right and wrong. Without an infinite being on which to base morality, there are simply no absolutes. So, when an atheist claims that something is right or wrong, questioning "why" often results in an interesting discussion.

Utilitarianism

"The utilitarian position argues that long-range consequences determine what is right and what is wrong."[5] Therefore an action is not good in and of itself; it is good only if there are beneficial results from that act. For instance, the firemen and police officials who ran into the twin towers on 9/11 were brave men. Yet the utilitarian would say that the act of entering those doomed buildings was only good if they saved some lives while doing it. For instance, if one of the men entered the building with the intention of helping, but got bewildered by the smoke and ended up not helping anyone, then the action was not a "good act." Remember, it is not the intention or motivation that makes an action "good" or "bad," it is the results of this action which determines its excellence.

[5] Geisler and Feinberg, *Introduction to Philosophy*, 389.

Like pragmatism, the crux of the problem revolves around who determines what is "good" and what consequences are better than others. Some like Jeremy Bentham (1748–1832) say that pleasures are all equal, and whatever produces the most pleasure in the most people is the best choice to make. John Stuart Mill (1806–1873), argues that certain satisfactions, like intellectual and sophisticated pleasures, are of a higher quality than mere fleshly desires. Yet the utilitarianists will never successfully answer the question of what is "good" due to the fact that each of us have our own opinions of what is a "good result." For instance, in the issue discussed above with Rahab and the spies, most utilitarians would argue that Rahab should have lied because it caused the better result for her (she was saved from death). Yet Jeremy Bentham may have disagreed because there were likely more people in Jericho than there were Jews. And since Rahab's action contributed to the demise of the people of Jericho, the decision caused pain in the majority of the people involved. Since most of the people were harmed by the lie, he would have said it was the wrong action. Thus, just like pragmatism, we are left with individuals determining goodness subjectively; and this ends in relativism.

Ethical Relativism

Jean-Paul Sartre once said, "There was nothing left in heaven, no right or wrong, nor anyone to give me orders . . . I am doomed to have no other law but mine . . . . For I . . . am a man, and every man must find his own way."[6] Some people believe that there is no "right or wrong" or absolute laws that can be applied to all people. Ethical relativism suffers from the same pitfalls as the subjective view of truth discussed in chapter three. If we took this ethical standard to its logical end, our society would end in anarchy and everyone would do whatever they like. Prisons would be emptied and mental asylums would go out of business. In reference to our Rahab illustration, the relativist would say that Rahab made the right decision only if Rahab thought she made the right decision. It is solely Rahab's opinion that counts.

Conventionalism

Conventionalism, or cultural relativism, is the concept that "right and wrong" are merely determined by the culture in which a person lives.

[6] Jean-Paul Sartre, "The Flies," in *No Exit and Three Other Plays* (New York: Collier-Macmillan, 1966), 121–23.

Simply put, your view of ethics is dependent on your environment. Therefore, if you were brought up to believe that homosexuality is wrong, then that would be your perspective. While there is some truth that your environment affects your perspective, conventionalists argue that you are determined to believe what your culture or sub-culture believes. You are subconsciously forced to uphold the ethical system of your environment.

While there are certain things that are cultural "conventions" such as which side of the street to drive on and the age at which people are able to drive, claiming that ALL ethical claims are conventional is counterintuitive. First, you have many cultures and even subcultures that have conflicting ethical systems. Consider a child whose parents have completely different worldviews. What if his mother was a theist and father was an atheist? You also have entire cultures split down the middle on certain issues like abortion and capital punishment. How does conventionalism solve these problems?

Secondly, if conventionalism were true, one nation, or a group of countries like the United Nations, would never have the right to look upon a culture and claim that what they were doing was "wrong." The United States could never step in and stop what another culture was doing. What if a country still practiced human sacrifice? What if a dictator was sporadically killing his own people? What right would we have, under conventionalism, to deem their ethical standards corrupt and assert that we need to take action?

In Rahab's situation, a conventionalist would argue that her actions simply depended on the culture in which she lived. Therefore, if those in Jericho felt lying was acceptable, then her action was moral.

The Theistic View of Ethics

While three different types of ethical systems will be considered here, all of them have a critical similarity: absolute truth. Each of these systems holds as their foundation the concept that there are "rights and wrongs" that can be applied to all people and all cultures. This ethical system is not a product of man, or even nature, but flows from our morally perfect God. God is infinitely loving, or omnibenevolent, and he is the foundation by which all ethical claims are justified.

The only apparent flaw in the theistic view of ethics arises when there is a true ethical dilemma; the only choices that can be made seem to be evil. These are situations where one cannot even ask "What would Jesus do?" due to the fact that Jesus is all-powerful and could get out of any situation he wished. So, if Jesus was in Rahab's situation, he could have miraculously transported the spies out of Jericho and told the soldiers that the spies were no longer there (then it would have been the truth!). While the three ethical systems below have an important similarity, the focus of the discussion below deals with the different ways they handle ethical dilemmas.

Absolutism

The majority of theists, whether Christian, Jew, Muslim, or otherwise, are absolutists. You have likely been brought up to believe in absolutism, and just like all the other systems, it has strengths and weaknesses.

Basically, absolutism states that there are absolute laws that should never be broken in ANY situation. Saint Augustine dedicated two works to this system, called *On Lying* and *Against Lying*, where he discussed that it was never right to lie, even if it resulted in a saved life or someone becoming a Christian.

Absolutism has at its core an understanding that God's providence should be trusted, and if a difficult situation arises, the best bet is to simply follow God's rules no matter the consequence. While trusting God is of supreme importance in the Christian faith, the problem is that there were definitely times in Biblical history where if this concept were followed, Christianity would probably not even exist! For instance, Abraham deceived an Egyptian Pharaoh[7] and later the King of Gerar[8] to spare his wife's life. If these kings had killed Sarah or Abraham, the Jewish nation would have never been produced. Again, if Rahab had not lied, the Jewish nation may not have overtaken the town of Jericho, and they may have never reached Canaan.

Lastly, absolutists deny that there has ever been a situation that exemplifies a true ethical dilemma. For instance, in the situation of Rahab, there is no ethical conflict; Rahab should have simply not sinned. Telling the truth or not answering at all would have been a proper response. Yes, not answering at all would have been acceptable under this system; yet sometimes this does not work. For instance, there are two situations in the Bible where people made oaths in the name of God and where a "true ethical dilemma" cannot be denied. David, in 1 Samuel 25 makes the oath to kill Nabal and all of his men. Jephthah made an oath in Judges 11 to sacrifice his daughter to God. One of these men fulfilled his oath, and the other did

---

[7] Gen. 12:10–20.

[8] Gen. 20:1–2.

not.[9] Whether they kept the oath or not, doing nothing here would not have helped the situation. This is a true ethical dilemma for which the absolutist must give an answer. Should Jephthah have sacrificed his innocent daughter, or broken his oath to God? What would you have done?

Conflicting and Graded Absolutism

Both conflicting and graded absolutism argue that there are true ethical dilemmas that we need to take into account. Due to our finite nature and the corrupt world we live in, it is possible to get in situations that seem to create serious ethical problems. Remember that both of these systems believe in absolutes, and in normal circumstances they look just like absolutism. Yet, when ethical problems arise, these two systems attempt to solve the problem.

Conflicting and Graded Absolutism have been grouped together due to the fact that they both rest on the same foundation: a hierarchy of moral laws. To explain, consider this question: Are all sins the same? Are all good acts equally good? These two systems argue that the Bible demonstrates that moral acts are not of equal weight. While it is true that all sins separate us from God, there is no doubt that God treats different sins with different punishments.

Most who oppose this view quote sources such as Matthew 5:28, where Jesus seemed to argue that lusting "in your heart" is just as bad as the actual act of adultery. Yet in that same passage, Jesus cites different punishment for different acts. In Matthew 5:22 Jesus states, "But I tell you that anyone who is angry with his brother will be subject to judgment. Again, anyone who says to his brother, 'Raca,' is answerable to the Sanhedrin. But anyone who says, 'You fool!' will be in danger of the fire of hell." Does it seem here that Jesus is judging certain sins as worse than others and deserving of harsher punishment? In another instance, Jesus states as a fact that there are greater and lesser evils. In a discussion with Pilate Jesus says that, "the one who handed me over to you is guilty of a greater sin."[10]

This sort of hierarchy even boils over to what will happen in the afterlife. For those who have done greater evils receive greater punishment (Romans 2:6 Psalm 62:12; Prov. 24:12; Rev. 20:12) and those who have done the greater goods receive a bigger reward (Matt. 5:12; Matt. 6:6; Luke 6:35; Eph. 6:8). But should this even be a surprise to us? Is not God

---

[9] Eccl. 5:4 emphatically states that if you make a vow to God, you must fulfill it!

[10] John 19:11.

a just God? For instance, if I caught two students doing different sins, one cheating and the other chewing gum in class, would I punish them equally? And for that matter, would it be fair to expel the gum chewer? Of course, in God's eyes we are all sinners who deserve punishment,[11] but would it seem fair that Hitler and an ethical non-Christian receive the same exact eternal penalty for their actions?

Conflicting absolutism and Graded absolutism are very similar except for their treatment of conflicting ethical situations. First, **conflicting absolutism** argues that in these situations we should choose "the lesser of two evils." Some argue that sin is a sin and there is no way around it, so we should simply choose the sin that is a lesser evil. One of the two problems with this view is that would seem that in an ethical dilemma we would be morally required to do an immoral act. In other words, in order to do the "right thing," you would have to sin! Secondly, this view seems to contradict God's Word. In 1 Corinthians 10:13, Paul writes that "God is faithful; he will not let you be tempted beyond what you can bear. But when you are tempted, he will also provide a way out so that you can stand up under it." Yet, if you *must sin* in these dilemmas, then God *has not* provided a way out! And since God must punish sin, then you are, in fact, culpable for the sin you just committed; even though you had to sin! Therefore, Conflicting Absolutism solves the problems of normal absolutism, yet it has problems of its own.

Graded absolutism simply perceives these ethical dilemmas from the opposite perspective. Instead of choosing a lesser evil, we are required to choose the greater good. In graded absolutism, when a person chooses the greater good, it is not a sin. For instance, Rahab's dilemma was this: "I either have the option of being honest and upholding truth, or the option of preserving life." Thus truth and life were the two moral goods that were her alternatives. Since life is of a higher moral quality than truth, Rahab choose the greater good and was rewarded by God. Thus, Rahab's lie was not a sin. This concept takes care of the problem of ethical dilemmas, while not falling into the problems of conflicting absolutism.

In another example, it even seems that God endorses the concept of graded absolutism. In Ezra 10 the Israelites had made the horrendous mistake of marrying pagan spouses and therefore indulging in a pagan lifestyle. Ezra, a prophet of God, assembled the Israelites and said, "You have been unfaithful; you have married foreign women, adding to Israel's guilt. Now make confession to the Lord, the God of your fathers, and do his

---

[11] Rom. 3:23.

will. Separate yourselves from the peoples around you and from your foreign wives."[12] Thus the prophet of God said that it was God's will that they divorce their wives. While there is no doubt that God "hates divorce,"[13] we must be able to explain why God told Ezra to break what seemed to be an absolute moral law. This seems to be a true ethical dilemma. The Jews either had to break the covenant of marriage (Gen. 2:24) or continue to break the law concerning marrying unbelievers (Neh. 13:25–26). Were they to remedy the situation by divorce? God, who spoke through the mouth of his prophet Ezra, apparently felt that a proper marriage to fellow Israelites was a greater moral good than the actual institution of marriage.[14]

As a last and more poignant illustration, remember how you felt when you saw the images on the television screen depicting the tragic events that occurred during Hurricane Katrina. Americans watched with disbelief when many of the victims rushed grocery stores to pilfer all their contents. Now of course there were people who took things that they did not need, but if you were in that situation and your family was to the point of starvation would you be one of those people who took bread and water? Here again we have a true dilemma. Of course, God tells us not to steal throughout the Bible, but Paul tells Timothy in 1 Tim. 5:8, "If anyone does not provide for his relatives, and especially for his immediate family, he has denied the faith and is worse than an unbeliever." So, what is a Christian to do? Again, in this situation it seems that the moral quality of life is greater than that of truth.

Summary

As discussed throughout the book, one of the biggest problems with naturalistic worldviews is that they simply do not have grounds for ethics. Why do naturalists behave the way they do? If they answered honestly they would have to answer "impulses and opinions." For if there is no absolute truth or absolute morality, then they only depend on themselves for their moral grounding. Maybe you realized as you read through the naturalists' positions on ethics, that each of their ideas stemmed from the views of truth we discussed earlier. It seems that utilitarianism resembles pragmatism, ethical relativism comes from the subjective view of truth, and conventionalism/cultural relativism is a result of the coherence view of

---

[12] Ezra 10:10–11.

[13] Mal. 2:16.

[14] See a completely different context in 1 Cor. 7; for more information see Geisler and Howe's *When Critics Ask*, 215.

truth. The arguments against these views are very similar to their predecessors and none of them end in absolute truth or absolute morality.

Lastly, three different views of absolutism were covered. While which is correct is not as essential to Christianity as the resurrection of Christ, it still should be thoroughly discussed. Realize that this is certainly an area where Christians can disagree and still remain united under our Lord Jesus. Yet to do this amicably, we must remember to maintain our opinion with "gentleness and respect."[15]

Study Questions

1. What is ethics and why do you think we should study it?
2. Before you read the chapter, which view of ethics did you believe? Have you changed your view after reading the chapter?
3. Given the account of Rahab, do you believe that lying was the right thing to do? What would you have done in that situation?
4. In chart form, write how Rahab would have reacted if she assumed utilitarianism, relativism, conventionalism, absolutism, conflicted absolutism, and graded absolutism. Would she lie or tell the truth? Why?

Terms to Consider

Ethics
Utilitarianism
Ethical Relativism
Conventionalism
Absolutism
Conflicting Absolutism
Graded Absolutism

Memory Verse Options

Micah 6:8

Going Beyond the Call of Duty: Readings for the Overachiever

Beckwith, Francis J. *Do the Right Thing: Readings in Applied Ethics and Social Philosophy*. Stamford: Wadsworth Publishing, 2001.

Clark, David and Robert Rakestraw ed. *Readings in Christian Ethics: Issues and Applications*. Grand Rapids: Baker Books, 1996.

Geisler, Norman. *Christian Ethics*. Grand Rapids: Baker Books, 1993.

[15] 1 Pet. 3:15.

Geisler, Norman and Thomas Howe. *When Critics Ask*. Grand Rapids: Baker Books, 1992.

Lewis, C. S. *Mere Christianity.* Nashville: Broadman and Holman, 1980.

Chapter 13

Apologetics and Evangelism

"How, then, can they call on the one they have not believed in? And how can they believe in the one of whom they have not heard? And how can they hear without someone preaching to them?" [1]

—The Apostle Paul

Introduction

Mark Cahill, a passionate evangelist and youth speaker writes, "Three hundred million years from now, the only thing that will matter is who is in heaven and who is in hell. And if that is the only thing that will matter then, that should be one of our greatest concerns now." [2] He makes a great point. After all is said and done and our lives are over, all that is left is our place with God. There will be some who will enjoy heaven forever, and others who will be banished to an eternity without God.

Arguably one of the most dramatic and heart-wrenching Hollywood scenes appears in the movie *Schindler's List*. Oskar Schindler was a savvy German businessman who lived during the time of the holocaust. He began using Jews as workers for his factory, and slowly realized that if he bargained with the Germans to get more Jews, he would essentially be saving their lives. Toward the end of the movie, Oskar was preparing to leave the Jews at the conclusion of the war. Suddenly, he began to uncontrollably weep. He looked at his fancy car, nice watch, and gold jewelry and realized that he could have helped even more Jews escape the hands of the treacherous Nazi regime. Even though he had helped over one thousand Jewish men and women, Oskar Schindler knew he could have done more.

---

[1] Rom. 10:14.

[2] Mark Cahill, *One Thing You Can't Do in Heave* (Dallas: Biblical Discipleship Ministries, 2002), 11.

The implication here is simple. In 2 Corinthians 5:10 it is written that we will all "appear before the judgment seat of Christ." Can you imagine what that will be like? Of course, all of us will be ashamed because every one of us is sinful, but will you regret that you have not shared Christ with all of those loved ones around you? What could you say to Jesus to explain why you haven't told others about his love? While our time on earth is precious and there is no doubt that we should live life to the fullest while under God's standards, each of us must consider what place evangelism has in our Christian walk.

Why Don't We Witness?

While many people justify their lack of evangelism due to the fact they haven't been "called" to witness, this idea is not backed up in Scripture. There are those in the Bible who were called for a specific purpose such as missionary work and serving those who are in need; but each and every one of us should be looking for ways to let others know about the love of Christ. While we can agree that some people have been better trained and equipped for such a task, none of us can claim that we are so unequipped that we should not even try! Jesus commands us to "go and make disciples of all nations, baptizing them in the name of the Father and of the Son and of the Holy Spirit, and teaching them to obey everything I have commanded you."[3]

There seem to be three reasons why a Christian would not evangelize. They have been summarized here as **faith, fear, and foolishness**.

Unfortunately, some of us lack the faith to share what we believe. Evangelism simply should be the "overflow of our hearts."[4] As mentioned earlier in this book, "One's whole life revolves around what he believes to be real." Yet if Christ's love is real, why don't we share it with our friends? Some of us simply lack the faith to evangelize. This may be an extremely bold assertion, but if you aren't even interested in the eternal destiny of your neighbor, maybe this is due to the fact that your belief in the afterlife is not as strong as it could be.

I personally struggled with this in college. I did not have a strong enough faith to evangelize to my friends. Why you ask? I was afraid that Christianity might have been wrong. In high school I toyed with the idea that I would eventually become a youth pastor. One of my worst nightmares during that time went something like this: I take a group of young

---

[3] Matt. 28:19.

[4] Matt. 12:34.

people to a church camp, but on the way the bus flips and we all go to meet our maker. On reaching the pearly gates Muhammad greets us at the door and says, "Who are you guys?" Honestly, seeing Muhammad in heaven was frightening, but more disconcerting was the terror on the faces of the young people who came to me for guidance. Until I truly believed that the Christian faith was and is real, I did not feel comfortable sharing about my relationship with Christ.

Secondly, many of us are simply scared to bring up our faith. How are your friends going to react? What if they say that you are crazy? While you may fear losing your "cool" status with friends, remember that your discussions about faith may be the only chance for them to hear about Christianity from a respected friend. If your discussions are peppered with humility, care, and respect, your friend should respond in kind. But what if the friend rejects the message? Simply know that God will bless you for your actions, even when the person does not accept Christ. Paul writes in 1 Corinthians 6–8, "I planted the seed, Apollos watered it, but God made it grow. So neither he who plants nor he who waters is anything, but only God, who makes things grow. The man who plants and the man who waters have one purpose, and each will be rewarded according to his own labor." Of course, you want to keep this friendship alive, because now this friend knows that you are a person who can answer questions about Christianity if he has them. Many times people need to deliberate about Christianity for weeks, sometimes even years, before God moves their hearts and they begin their journey towards Christ.

Lastly, sometimes we are simply too lazy, self-centered, or busy to think of the spiritual struggles of our neighbors. Whether a teenager, young adult, or even a full-grown individual, we all understand what it means to be hurried and overwhelmed with life. Unfortunately this sometimes leads us to be ignorant of our friends' eternal destiny. Of course, this is why this section is called "foolishness." This ignorance, like most forms of foolishness, is usually not intentional, but this does not lesson the problems. Your friends may die without Christ. How do we rid ourselves of this ignorance? It seems that unless we can intentionally work on our walk with Christ, then the gospel will not be shared. If you can purposely read your Bible, not due to a class assignment, but because you want to draw closer to the heart of God, then there will be a positive change in the Christian Church toward evangelism. Until we can all pray with the intention of speaking to God personally, and not merely publicly, only then will there be a personal, internal revolution in our souls. This may sound weird, but as it is with most relationships, until we can work out our relationship with God nothing else will work out right. Personally, when my relationship with God is strong, these are the times when evangelism comes easy, almost second nature.

What if They Don't Accept?

In order to be ready for your friends' reactions, you need to be ready to answer any question or concern that they may have about Christianity.[5] These reactions to Christianity can be categorized into three kinds: **denial, dislike, and disinterest.**

The first of these three is the one we have dealt with through much of this book. If a person **denies** the facts of Christianity, then apologetics needs to be utilized. If the person is an atheist, we should attempt to demonstrate God's existence. If he is a polytheist, we should carefully critique the concept of multiple finite Gods. If he is a Jew, we should lovingly explain how Jesus was and is the Christ. While "denial" is the most intellectually challenging of the three, we must remember that any barrier that stands between the person and God must be removed before they will take the gospel seriously.

The second category is on a completely different level. Sometimes individuals have bad experiences in church, or have been treated poorly by a person who called himself a Christian. They simply **dislike** the way Christianity has been portrayed. It could be something as silly as the style of music that a church plays in worship or as critical as a person being mistreated by a pastor. In these sorts of situations your reaction depends on the specifics of the incident. If the person went to church once and didn't like the worship, then you may need to inform them that there are many different types of worship and invite them to your church or another church that you think would be appropriate. The more serious problems may take more time and care. Issues such as hypocrisy, betrayal, and spiritual neglect may be mentioned, but the fact of the matter is that the best thing you can do for this person is be the true Christian that he expected in the first place. Pray for him, befriend him and help resolve these issues; all of this to attempt to introduce him to your caring Christian community and eventually to Christ Himself.

Lastly, there are those who would claim that they are **disinterested** in spiritual matters. They don't go to church or pray to God. They usually claim that they don't even care. While their actions show indifference, just know that EVERYONE cares about what happens to them after they die.

---

[5] 1 Pet. 3:15.

Even if the person is an agnostic (and thus you would have to refer back to the denial section), he still has an opinion about what happens to his body after he dies.

Since most Americans do believe that there is a God and an afterlife,[6] you have to wonder if this person's claim that "I don't care" is merely a clever strategy to get you to move on to another topic. Of course, listen to the Holy Spirit on this issue, but a decent reply to his claim is to merely call his bluff, "You mean that you don't care about what happens after you die?" If he responds by continuing to say that he doesn't care, you probably should begin to wonder what has happened in his life to make him feel so dejected. A good reply would be, "Well, I care enough about you that I am concerned about what happens to you." With this sentence you have hit two birds with one stone. You have expressed your care for your friend and shown that you are specifically worried about their afterlife. Again, if these claims of indifference are not a strategy, and this person is really despondent, continued expressions of concern will likely result in deeper discussions and maybe even a deeper friendship. While there are no "perfect sentences" to say to a friend who simply doesn't care, the best course of action is to be that good friend and to spend countless hours in prayer before the throne of our Glorious Father.

What if They Want to Accept Christ as Their Savior?

I personally believe that one of the most important things that a Christian should know is how to lead a friend to Christ. There are many styles and tools that Christians can use to demonstrate Christ's love, and you should feel free to find one that suits your style. The one that will be used here is the famous **bridge illustration**. You can do this presentation anywhere as long as you have a pen or pencil and a napkin (or any other paper). There will be a total of four verses used with this illustration, so it would be helpful if these were memorized. Start with a picture like this:

[6] In the USA, 92% Believe in a God and 85% believe in heaven, Opinion Dynamics Corporation survey, taken from Foxnews.com story entitled "More Believe in God than in Heaven," June 18, 2004.

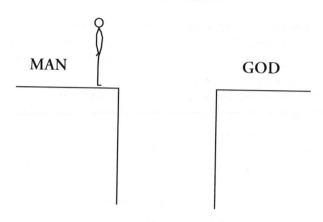

Most Christians know John 3:16, and this is a great verse with which to start, but don't say the whole thing! Start with merely "For God so loved the world." These six words are a great starting point because they reveal that the God of Christianity is a good God and wants to have a loving relationship with each individual. Thus, the Christian God is NOT the God of deism; he is truly a God who wants a connection with the person with whom you are talking. But of course, there is a problem:

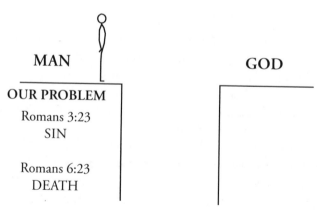

In Romans 3:23 Paul states that "all have sinned and fall short of the glory of God." Basically, because we are imperfect and have sinned, our relationship with God is impossible. Sin is like a chasm or a huge rift that has separated us from God. This is the gap between "man" and "God" in the illustration. Because God is completely pure and holy, he cannot have an intimate relationship with a sinning creature. To illustrate this, imagine pouring a pot of melted, dirty gold into a pot of pure gold. What do you get?, dirty gold. That is the problem. As a pure being, God cannot personally bond with us.

Due to this disconnection, the ultimate result is physical and spiritual death. Romans 6:23 reads, "For the wages of sin is death, but the gift of God is eternal life in Christ Jesus our Lord." The point you are trying to make here is simply that we have a choice either to spend eternity in a place where we can have a relationship with God, or a place where we will be separated from God.

GOD'S PURPOSE
John 3:16   ETERNAL LIFE

MAN   **GOD**

OUR PROBLEM

Romans 3:23
SIN

Romans 6:23
DEATH

Ephesians 2:8–9
NOT WORKS

ETERNAL DEATH

Many people believe the unfounded notion that doing good works will bring us into favor with God. In your discussion with your friend, ask him to name some examples of good actions. Then draw bridges that only make it halfway across the chasm, and label these as "good actions" or maybe even draw multiple bridges and label them with the same "good actions" that your friend listed. The idea that we can do good works to get to heaven is not found in the Bible. The fact of the matter is that our works, no matter how good, cannot completely remove the sin that has infected our lives. In Ephesians 2:8–9 Paul emphasizes "For it is by grace you have been saved, through faith—and this not from yourselves, it is the gift of God— not by works, so that no one can boast." The point is that only God himself can eliminate the penalty and stain of sin in our lives and bring us into a relationship with him. With this in mind, God sent his only son to die, so that He could pay the ultimate price for the sins of humanity. Through his life, death, and resurrection, we can be assured that if we believe in him, we will spend eternity with God.

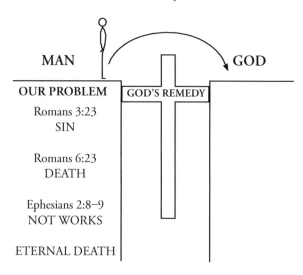

To conclude your presentation, draw the cross and read John 3:16 completely "For God so loved the world that he gave his one and only Son, that whoever believes in him shall not perish but have eternal life." Of course, the thought that should enter into your friend's mind should be "Well, how do I do this? How do I begin this relationship with God?" You probably remember that when you became a Christian you prayed a prayer, and you maybe have heard many different versions of this prayer since you have been saved. The specific words of the prayer aren't as important as the subject matter that needs to be addressed. Don't be afraid, you can make up the exact words of the prayer on the spot, but make sure that you mention these things:

1. Acknowledge that the person has sinned, is sorry for these sins, and realizes that he is separated from God.

2. That he wants to accept God's free gift of salvation that is a result of Jesus' sacrifice on the cross.
3. And they want to begin a relationship with God through his son Jesus.
4. (optional)—Thank God for this opportunity.

Summary

While many Christians do not acknowledge their own responsibility to evangelize to the world, there is no doubt of Jesus' intention that his followers should spread his message. We should all take a hard look at our walk with Christ to see if we have barriers that keep us from sharing the gospel. Even more specifically, we should pray for God to reveal to whom he would like us to share the gospel.

Realize that people usually don't become a Christian after the first time they hear the gospel. Like any other major decision, they need to ask questions, think it over and decide on their own. You should do your best to keep in touch with your friend in order to answer any questions or simply to remind them that you care about them. Don't forget that you also must also give the Holy Spirit time to do his work and draw your friend to Him.

Study Questions

1. If you have shared the gospel with someone, explain the results of this encounter. Did the person become a Christian? If not, what kept him from accepting Christ?
2. Did you accept Christ the first time you heard the message of the Gospel? How long did it take you to decide to follow him?
3. Come up with your own version of the sinner's prayer incorporating all four of the essential elements as listed above.

Memory Verses for this section

John 3:16
Romans 3:23
Romans 6:23
Ephesians 2:8–9

More optional verses

Matthew 28:19
2 Corinthians 5:10

Going Beyond the Call of Duty: Readings for the Overachiever

Cahill, Mark. *One Thing You Can't Do in Heaven.* Dallas: Biblical Discipleship Ministries, 2002.

Comfort, Ray. *How to Win Souls and Influence People.* Gainsville: Bridge-Logos Publishers, 1999.

Hybels, Bill and Mark Mittelberg. *Becoming a Contagious Christian.* Grand Rapids: Zondervan, 1996.